BROAD STREET

A Guide to investing in the Nigerian Stock Market

Broad Street: A Guide to Investing in the Nigerian Stock Market

By Adewale Dada

Copyright 2006

All rights reserved by the author. No part of this publication can be reproduced, stored in a retrieval system, or transmitted in any form or by any means, without the explicit and prior permission of the author.

DISCLAIMER
The author is a financial journalist and not registered to provide brokerage or investment advisory services. While the author attempts to ensure the accuracy and compliancy of the contents in this book for its intended purpose, errors or omissions may occur due to circumstances beyond the control of the author. The contents are in no way construed as an offer for the purchase or sale of securities in any jurisdiction and in this regard, the author claims non-liability for the presentation or misrepresentation of facts in this book. The author recommends that you independently research any investment before making a financial decision and inform yourself of the risks involved; including seeking expert counsel from a financial advisor. There exists risk in trading financial instruments, past results are not indicative of future results. The author assumes no responsibility for your trading or investment results.

ISBN 978-1-84728-509-6

TABLE OF CONTENTS

ACKNOWLEDGEMENTS	vi
INTRODUCTION	vii
CHAPTER 1: Hey dude, where is Nigeria?	11
CHAPTER 2: The Birth of Broad Street	27
CHAPTER 3: The Nigerian Stock Market	45
CHAPTER 4: Finding the money to invest	57
CHAPTER 5: Research, research and some more research!	69
CHAPTER 6: Selecting a Stockbroker	89
CHAPTER 7: Managing the Nigerian Factor	101
CHAPTER 8: Survival tips for investors	115
APPENDIX	125

ACKNOWLEDGEMENTS

It would be easier for me to give general thanks to everyone involved in the conception and birth of this book, but I fear some 'good friends' would do me harm if I don't spell out their names! So here we go. First and foremost, I owe huge thanks to the Almighty who gives us the intellect to share information that profits mankind. Special thanks to the Chief Technology Officer of SEEDS Communications and Technologies, Steve Bolaji, whose expertise were immense during the design and editing phases, Peju Adelakun of Counters Trust Securities who provided vital research, and Chinedum who redirected his attention from more important tasks to focus his journalistic and editing skills on polishing my clumsy drafts into a script that actually makes sense.

It would be illegal to not single out an old friend who challenged me to write a book years ago; Kola Owolabi, I finally did it baby! My literary cheerleaders Joyce and Jenn, thanks for the 'I promise to buy your book when you're done' moments. Let me single out Folake Bukoye, who not only inspired me during a tough period but also prayed for me. You're one of the good ones. Special thanks to my mum who always had money to buy a book for me no matter how hard times were, you have a special place in my heart. Dad, you are a total geek still living in denial but I love you for it! To my siblings Nike, Sade and Leke, thanks for your support.

There are many out there whose questions at seminars and in informal discussions, sparked the intellectual challenge for me to overcome my fear of writing a book that could help others participate in the Nigerian economic revolution. To you all, I am appreciative in ways words can not muster. Finally, I have to thank you the reader for holding this book in your hands right now and giving it more than a brief glance. I hope that its contents add value to you in ways that exceed the financial realm. Any errors found are strictly mine. Once again, thanks to everyone who made *Broad Street* a reality.

INTRODUCTION

Nine hundred seconds was all it took to give birth to what you are holding in your hands right now. During a very inadequate 15 minute break from one of the most boring accounting classes I had ever taken in my MBA program, a friend and I had jumped into a computer lab to check out stock prices. You see, my friend happened to be a Master investor, although he had that very "broke college student, I can't help myself" thing about him which masked the fact that he was making a killing in stocks listed on the electronic stock exchange, NASDAQ. NASDAQ just so happens to be one of the largest stock exchanges in the United States and my friend had positioned himself in some of the most profitable biotechnology companies in the country and was reaping an almost illegal profit! I watched the bold smile on his face broaden as the computer monitor streamed financial data that seemed to be singing a tune that only he had the privilege to dance to. Lucky guy, I thought.

As he zigzagged from one financial website to the other, I turned away to focus on my stock portfolio to see if it would play me a lullaby and make me even with this lucky nuisance I had as a friend. My eyes widened as I watched my portfolio hold steady over the past forty-eight hours, gaining only 2% in the past week. Normally, I would be downcast at such returns but on the other hand, I guess it was the market telling me to slow down. After all, I had gained a 357% return on a little bank stock less than a year ago and was still reaping the dividends of that investment. No, I did not make that money on the New York Stock Exchange, NASDAQ or any of the more popular boards here in the United States. It all happened on a stock exchange thousands of miles away in the city of Lagos, Nigeria's largest city and home to the Nigerian Stock Exchange - one of the fastest growing stock markets in the world. As the ticker on my screen spat out the stock prices of various Nigerian companies, my friend slid over, peered at the screen intently for about a minute, looked at me for a split second, looked at the screen again, turned his chair full circle and asked me the most amazing question I had ever heard in my professional life: "Does Nigeria have a stock market"?

The question seemed strange since I was under the impression that everyone would know that Nigeria was the largest economy in Africa with multibillion dollar industries and 'should' have a stock exchange. However, I was wrong and my friend had enlightened me on the apparent lack of information on business and finance available to people outside Nigeria and indeed, Africa. Most people, who have an impression about Africa, usually have a dire picture painted in their memory of squalid living conditions, poor healthcare, the ravage of AIDS and other bleak situations. However, there is another side to the continent that the global community does not see. It is the emergence of a budding class of entrepreneurs across the continent, huge corporations that supply the essential energy needs of ordinary households in Europe, Asia and the Americas, the comparatively stable economic policies that are creating a sustainable middle class, the continent's vibrant capital markets stretching from Johannesburg to Lagos and much more. The interesting thing about the economic revolution in Africa is that Nigeria is at the forefront of that change. The stock market in the country has been a significant trigger of that change, amassing great funds for challenging and profitable projects, making millionaires out of many investors. In the past decade, returns on equity investing in Africa and Nigeria in particular have significantly outpaced returns that can be found in the United States or the emerging Asian giants - India and China. As I pondered these thoughts, my friend tapped me and pointed at the clock. "Oh God, back to boring ACCT 801- Managerial Accounting", I thought and headed back to class.

    The following day, I held a seminar on investing in Nigerian stocks on campus and had people mob me with questions on how to go about trading in this emerging economy. I guess my experience working in one of the largest brokerages in Nigeria did not hurt my new status as a "financial expert" (whatever that meant) amongst my new wannabe investor friends. However, I guess the challenge for me was getting my friends to start investing in Nigeria only when they had the facts backing their every investment move. As excited as I am to inform people on the huge opportunity that exists in Nigeria, particularly its stock market; I consider my primary objective as a financial journalist to educate my audience on taking the right steps that actually puts money in their pockets and protects them from the many pitfalls and shylocks that are ever present in the high stakes world of finance.

If you are like me and seem to find yourself controlled by some metaphysical force switching the channel to CNBC, you have no problem finding more than enough information on American based companies. Thousands of online and library resources are available for you to peruse and make fairly informed judgments on which companies are worthy of your hard-earned money. At the same time, if you seek information on the opportunity available in Nigeria and its stock market, you seem to be at a dead-end when it comes to finding the right information. This book aims to solve that problem. There is so little coverage of the Nigerian economy in the global media that severely stops millions from making money in a country where returns are extremely profitable for the bold and informed global investor. After reading this book, you will find yourself in a class of investors who actually know what they are doing when it comes to investing abroad, whether it is in Nigeria or another country. There are many books that tell you what countries and companies to invest in, what investment strategies to implement and a whole lot of other information that could make you delirious sooner than you can ever realize. I am glad to say that the book in your hands is not one of them. For those of you who can not stand graphs flying all over a book in the name of looking professional, all I can say is: "YOU ROCK BABY"!

This book was written in plain language to make you go ahead and invest without thinking that you are not financially savvy enough. If the truth be told, there is no such thing as a financial expert. As long as you understand basic trends in society, manage your money well, have access to quality information and have an unbiased mindset to investing; you will be just fine. Don't get too comfortable yet. We will touch on some technical matters, explore the ups and downs of investing in the Nigerian stock market and I will throw out terms that might send you scurrying for a financial dictionary for enlightenment, but at the end of reading this book, you will be so ahead of the game. As you thumb through the pages, I will introduce you to the important facets of investing in Nigeria. You will share the history of the country, its politics and economy, financial system, the risk inherent in investing abroad and be provided with valuable information resources. I ask for your forgiveness in advance if some of the contents sound as boring as my accounting class but I prefer an informed investor to a stupid one who invests without the facts.

Although this book is targeted at American residents, investors elsewhere would find some of the tips helpful in their own investment journeys. Investing in a foreign country for some is an exciting experience, others find it daunting. No matter your investment personality, the information is always a guiding light that could make or break you. *Broad Street: a Simple Guide to Investing in the Nigerian Stock Market* is really a combination of the questions many of you asked me while I surveyed and conducted research for this book, and hopefully logical answers to those wonderful questions. I congratulate you on seeking information on the most exciting stock market in Africa and hope you take the time to engage in more research to improve on the knowledge that this book would bring you. That is the hallmark of a successful investor: cutting through the chaff and working with the facts.

Successful investing has always been and will remain an evolving form of self-education. It is my hope that this book educates, saves you time and energy; and ultimately aids you in achieving financial independence.

Chapter 1
Hey dude, where is Nigeria?

That was the question many people asked me when I moved to the United States in 2004. Apart from the fact that I was black and had a foreign accent, I could have being from Jamaica or Haiti (oh yeah, I got the Haitian one often) for all they cared. However, every now and then someone would recognize that I was from Nigeria and then the questions will start. "Where exactly is Nigeria?", "Do you wear clothes like we do here?", "Do you have roads and buildings?" The third question was my favorite to which I would reply: "Yes, we have roads. Actually, when the lights turn green, I go forward and when they turn red or yellow; the zebras and giraffes take their turn!" The reality of the Nigerian people and economy is very different from the perception many Americans have about it. In this chapter, we shall unveil the history and mystique of Nigeria to provide you with a clearer understanding of Nigeria's history and capability.

Everyday, millions of investors act on assumptions when it comes to investing abroad because of biased or even worse, false information. Imagine this: your broker calls to inform you of a hot emerging market fund for you to get into. You have no idea where your money is headed and if you do know the name of the country, your knowledge is limited to what *National Geographic* offers and what your broker tells you. Two reliable sources you think? Wrong! The famous orator, Marcus Cicero, once stated that "To remain ignorant of history is to remain a child". This chapter would take us back to the roots of Nigeria, the status of its economy and show you the main sectors that are driving the country's economic growth. The goal of this chapter is to provide you with a good idea of how Nigerian history plays a role in its economics and how your understanding of some historical facts enables you make well informed decisions when its time to trade. Many brokers call stocks in foreign companies "exotic" and mystify them so much that you find yourself either overtly intrigued by it or scared to death at transferring funds abroad. Come on, a stock is a stock. It goes up and it goes down, even if the company is quoted on the planet Mars!

ONCE UPON A TIME....

In 1914, the British colonial administration decided to amalgamate the southern and northern regions of the geopolitical area that is called Nigeria today. To mark that year as the origin of the Federal Republic of Nigeria would be a huge disservice to the rich history of the many peoples and cultures that exist within those boundaries. A few facts about this vast country would make you a historian in no time! Nigeria is the most populated African country with an estimated 138 million residents. With over 40 cities boasting populations exceeding a hundred thousand residents, the country is fast becoming an urbanized society, with less than half of its populace living in rural areas. Proud people, Nigerians would quickly let you know that one out of every six black persons walking the earth's surface is a Nigerian. But that is the Nigeria people know and talk about. The Nigeria with famous soccer players, massive oil and gas reserves, corrupt military governments, huge cities with poor infrastructure, imaginative scam letters, medical practitioners working around the world, and a volatile oil-rich Niger Delta. The Nigeria most people know is full of facts and fictions.

A quick history lesson on Nigeria could help you identify facts and aid your analysis of events in the country that could help you distinguish facts and understand the country's economic and political status in the twenty first century. You might be wondering, "What do my plans to buy Nigerian stocks have to do with the people or history?" A valid question no doubt and my answer is everything since people run everything, including your stock investments. As an old African proverb goes, "You can see what is coming by looking at what happened in the past". I guess many analysts will agree since that statement is in fact the bedrock of financial analysis, the ability to study historical data to predict future stock movements. Okay, so back to the whole colonial history thing we were talking about. Nigeria's boundaries are essentially the construct of its former British colonial rulers, who mapped the country in a manner that allowed them move commodities from the Northern hinterlands to the coastal ports in cities such as Lagos in Western Nigeria and Port Harcourt in the south, for export to the United Kingdom and other British colonies. This geopolitical caricature merged various ethnic groups that had very little in common, creating political and ethnic tensions that still affect the country till date. If you think running a country along Democratic or Republican party lines in the US is a daunting task, try governing a nation with over two hundred and fifty distinct ethnic-conscious groups! We will look at the major ethnic groups in the country, their history and the influence they wield in the modern-day Nigerian economy.

THE PEOPLE: CULTURE AND HISTORY

Nigerian cultural heritage can be traced as far back as 2,000 years ago when the *Nok* people in present-day Plateau State located in the Northern highlands developed a sophisticated iron fabrication industry and sculpted intricate terra-cotta household items. The region is dominated by the Hausa-Fulani ethnic stock (no pun intended!), with an estimated 43% of Nigerians living in this agriculturally fertile region. Since independence from England in 1960, the Hausas have held a grip on political power in Nigeria, producing seven of the country's twelve military and democratic leaders as at 2006. The region suffers a low level of education compared to other parts of the country. However, cheap labor, rich agricultural fields and the presence of valuable mineral resources has attracted food and mining companies to the region.

The Yoruba people represent a quarter of Nigerians and historical facts trace their history back to 1000 A.D. Early American and European slave merchants teamed up with unscrupulous Yoruba military commanders to chart the despicable and infamous slave trade. Historians attest to the fact that most African-Americans are of Yoruba descent due to the sheer size of the Yoruba Kingdom at the time. Today, Yoruba people maintain the highest literacy rates in Nigeria and are renowned technocrats in various industries. Due to the proximity of the region to the coast, most Nigerian and foreign companies locate their industrial operations in the area to facilitate exports to neighboring African countries, Europe and North America. Although they are the most educated and one of the most powerful blocs in the country that have produced great corporate titans such as Kase Lawal, founder of CAMAC International, the largest black owned energy services company in the United States, the region still lacks the entrepreneurial verve of the third largest ethnic bloc in Nigeria, the Igbos.

Known for their strong sense of individualism, Igbos can be found in the southeastern part of Nigeria. Before the advent of British colonial rule in Nigeria, Igbos had no central form of government and preferred the use of group votes to handle communal issues. For those who believe the tenets of democracy were formed in Europe, some research into the individualistic nature of Igbo society could be an eye opener! Although severely underrepresented in political administration at the national level, the Igbo community have channeled their energies and unparalleled business acumen into gaining strategic stakes in critical sectors of the Nigerian economy such as banking, industrial operations and transportation. Igbo businessmen engage in retail businesses in virtually every major African city and in fact, have the largest number of small businesses amongst Nigerians in the Diaspora.

HOW BRITISH BUSINESS TOOK OVER A NATION

The involvement of the British in Nigeria might sound irrelevant, even incompatible with your goals at making money in the Nigerian stock market but vital to your education. The British had been doing business with the various communities dotted along the Niger Delta region and the Yoruba merchants on the western frontier. With abundant natural resources, the region lying on and below the River Niger became the target of colonial powers such as France, Germany and England that held claim to other African states. The British suspicious of the intentions of European neighbors came up with the idea of cornering Nigeria for itself.

Sir George Goldie, a British entrepreneur and administrator with strong political connections in London, set about combining British business interests in the region under the umbrella of a mercantile company called the United African Company or UAC in 1879. In 1881, he was unsuccessful in receiving a charter from Downing Street to implement the empire building aspirations that were prevalent in Europe at the time. Luckily for him, the infamous Berlin Conference on Africa, where European countries gathered to carve Africa into European colonies, was convened in 1885 and Goldie who had in the interim period unscrupulously signed almost 400 political treaties with the chiefs of the lower Niger and Hausa states; was able to make a case on why Britain should have control over the area. In July 1886, after effectively buying out the French at the conference, a charter was accorded the UAC which was renamed the Royal Niger Company to control the region.

It was not too long before the territorial ambitions of the British were actualized. Considering the impracticality of a mere trading company competing with the neighboring state-supported protectorates of France and Germany, George Goldie went to England not to request a charter document but to close a deal that would firmly place the region under British control. On January 1, 1900, the Royal Niger Company transferred its territories to the British government for the sum of eight hundred and sixty-five thousand pounds sterling. Just like that, the ceded areas already under imperial control were mapped as the northern and southern protectorates of Nigeria. In 1914, the amalgamation of the two regions was completed. The representative of the Queen of England at the time, Lord Frederick Lugard did not know what to call the country; turned to his wife and asked for a suggestion. She pondered for a while, said "well, we control an area that surrounds the Niger River, so let's call it the Niger Area. Hey honey, I have a better idea- combine Niger and Area and you have Nigeria"! Of course, I dramatized the whole Madam Lugard monologue but you get my gist of how the country got its name.

For the next 25 years, the British had absolute control over their new subjects although pockets of violence occasionally erupted in the Northern and Southeastern regions. After World War II, a wave of nationalism swept over the African continent and Nigeria was right in its path. A war-weary England, badly bruised by the European war started redrawing its "empire" to fit its own borders as nationalist Nigerians demanded independence.

POST-COLONIAL NIGERIA

In 1960, the British acceded and granted Nigeria political autonomy. Three years after independence, the desire of the Nigerian political class to shed off any semblance of British influence on its ruling style caused the parliament to declare Nigeria a republic, styled after the American system of government which is more democratic, although that can be debatable in some quarters. With a federal form of government and new constitution, Nigeria was ready to power ahead with a wave of economic emancipation and political change across the continent. Oh boy, were they wrong. The post-independence era of Nigeria was and is still regarded as the most challenging period in the nation's history, as brutal ethnic conflicts brewed across the country as the many regions strived to exert their will over the other. Political rhetoric and ideology gave way to raw tribalism that prevented the country from implementing the policies that the first indigenous leaders had formulated to help the new nation gain economic strength. The problems were magnified by the obvious disparities in educational and economic levels between the relatively backward northern region and the seemingly progressive southern regions.

In 1966, two military coups set the precedent for strong ethnic sentiments that led to widespread violence and the eventual secession of the Igbo-dominated southeastern region from Nigeria. In May 1967, the Igbos led by an Oxford-educated soldier, Lieutenant Colonel Emeka Ojukwu, called the secessionist state *Biafra* and fought a bitter and bloody war with Federal forces for the next three years. On January 13, 1970, Biafran soldiers surrendered to Nigerian forces and the country was finally 'reunited'.

Over the next three decades, Nigerian has grappled with extensive military rule interspersed with brief relief under a democratic government between 1979 and 1983. Finally in 1999, Nigeria was able to conduct an election that was widely considered free but not necessarily fair and elect a government under the leadership of President Olusegun Obasanjo. To the credit of the Obasanjo administration, the country has gained a semblance of normalcy with the government paying attention to the basic problems that affect the Nigerian people such as the rehabilitation of abandoned infrastructure, instituting a sense of accountability and transparency in government, redeeming the country's negative human rights image and encouraging sustainable foreign investment. Despite remarkable improvements in the economic and political indices of the nation, sectarian violence occasionally breaks out between Christians and Muslims in northern Nigeria, while youth upheavals and kidnapping of foreigners no longer stun local residents in the impoverished oil-rich Niger Delta region.

THE NIGERIAN ECONOMY

After that harrowing but exciting history lesson (I can hear you gasp "What?!"), let us take some steps towards the Nigerian stock market with some information on the Nigerian economy, the largest in sub-Saharan Africa excluding South Africa. With the largest population of an African state and the largest segment of working Africans, Nigeria is indeed a giant on the African continent when it comes to the level of commercial activity and the number of small businesses owned. Its Gross Domestic Product (GDP) stood at $174.1 billion in 2005; roughly the size of the economy of the State of Arizona in the same period. During colonial times, the country had a vibrant agricultural and trading economy with the sector accounting for over 75% of national revenue. This is understandable since 95% of Nigeria's 92.4 million hectares of land area is assessed as suitable for cultivation.

With the discovery of oil in 1958, all that changed quickly as the sector was quickly abandoned with subsequent administrations paying little interest to agriculture while they were running around screaming, "I'm unbelievably rich baby"! Come on, of course they didn't do that in public. Government officials were too busy thinking on how to spend the billions of petrodollars international oil corporations were paying in royalty fees. With crisis in the middle-east and the cold war raging between the United States and the then communist Soviet Union, the geopolitical pendulum was swinging rapidly in the favor of oil producing countries. Nigeria was really having a ball.

Now a player in the global oil market, the country slowly slid into a subtle dependency on the oil sector. As the money poured in, the government invested in projects that did little to developing its industrial, scientific and human capacity but catered to the populist ideology of that era. The populace followed suit with a thirst for imported goods, draining foreign reserves that could have been placed in essential sectors like education, healthcare and industry. In fact, my parents told me that the money was flowing in so fast and in torrents, Nigerians were constantly traveling abroad on the weekends for no apparent reason and spending thousands of dollars on items that were not useful back home. Try that today with your retirement fund and the only place you will travel to is poverty lane! With the population growing fast and the agriculture sector neglected, Nigeria once an exporter of food became the single largest importer of food on the African continent. Now that oil had become the sole sustenance of the growing African giant, competition intensified amongst ethnic and regional blocs to gain power at the center so as to control the nation's oil wealth.

Subsequent military incursions in government, an unbridled level of corruption and poverty at unimaginable levels became the norm as oil prices crashed worldwide from the late 1970s into the mid-1980s. The Nigerian government started borrowing at incredulous rates and the foreign debt tanked at $32.2 billion on March 2001. An interesting thing to note is that the country had actually borrowed half of the amount but noncommittal military administrations had racked up amazingly high interest payment charges as oil prices fluctuated during the 1985-1996 period. Just like your favorite credit card company, foreign creditors such as the Paris and London Club of Creditors racked up those charges without batting an eye. Times were indeed tough for Nigerians as they saw their economy crumble from the earlier boom years. In such a catastrophic environment, many government officials started soliciting bribes from private citizens who wanted access to basic utilities such as electricity and telephone services, and job placements in vital government ministries and agencies. Today, many Nigerians will easily tell you that economic mismanagement is not the country's biggest problem but an endemic nature of corruption and nepotism.

After the 1999 election of President Olusegun Obasanjo, his administration focused on reviving the economy using respected technocrats and prudent fiscal policies. Two poverty-reduction strategies were initiated to combat corruption in the oil industry and build wealth for the over 55 million Nigerians estimated to live under the poverty line. One is the National Economic Empowerment and Development Strategy (NEEDS), a medium-to-long term economic reform agenda and the second, the Extractive Industries Transparency Initiative

(EITI) which is administered in part by the United Kingdom Department for International Development. Investments across the economic board have been relatively even as the government invested heavily in key sectors such as transportation, telecoms and food processing industries that could create value for local farmers. The tax regime is being revamped to attract importers to pay badly needed customs revenue. It is a well known fact that Nigerian importers would prefer smuggling in goods and services rather than pay the prohibitive tariffs imposed by government. To the credit of the Nigerian government, the economic indicators have swung favorably in the country's direction as world oil prices spiked to record highs between 2004 and 2006, with no end in sight as the Middle East struggles with crisis after crisis. As at May 2006, Nigeria had paid down its burdensome external debt and accumulated $34 billion in foreign exchange reserves. Not bad for a nation that had a negative balance just seven years earlier.

The changes in the structural segments of the economy are indicative that the country is headed for a new economic order if the nation's leadership remains focused on getting the country out of the doldrums and making it a viable investment destination for foreign investments and can convince millions of Nigerians living abroad to invest in their home country. Since 2000, the pace of foreign investment has picked up faster than at any other time in the history of the country and moribund sectors are now being targeted by the business community. As you structure your investment plan to include Nigerian stocks, I want you to be aware of key economic sectors that are correlated in some way to the stock exchange. Many of the large corporations that you will be investing in operate in these sectors, hiring millions of Nigerian citizens and critical to Nigerian economic policy from the formulation phase to implementation. Here are some of them.

Agriculture

Agriculture contributes 32% of Nigeria's national GDP and employs about 60% of the country's working population. As the fourth largest producer of cocoa in the world, Nigeria is an important partner in making your *Hershey*'s chocolate bar a decadent bundle of joy! The country is also the largest producer of cassava in the world, making it a viable feed source for millers in North America and Europe who were devastated by the deadly "Mad Cow" disease epidemic in the late 1990s and sought alternatives to wheat-based food components. With renewed government restructuring of the agricultural sector, it has grown by an estimated 2.9% annually between 2002 and 2004. Hopes are high that the groundnut and palm oil industries will pick up. Opportunity in the fishery industry is high as Nigerians worried about the avian flu affecting their poultry livestock have increased fish intake to record consumption levels. Aquaculture production is still very low and the country imports half of its fish needs. Some publicly traded multinational corporations, some in partnership with Nigerian entrepreneurs, operate plantations that provide rubber and grains that feed tire making and brewery companies. The greatest challenge for farmers in the country is access to rural credit as fluctuating but high interest rates have scared them away from the sector.

Oil and Gas

Nigeria is the eight largest producer of oil in the world with proven reserves of 25 billion barrels and natural gas reserves well in excess of 120 trillion cubic feet. With such resources, the country has earned an estimated $280 billion in cash receipts since the first oil well was drilled in 1958 but economists believe only 34% of those funds have actually contributed to economic development. With the United States being Nigeria's largest oil client with 8% of imports coming from the country, Nigeria is always on the radar of stock market analysts in Europe and America. Since the return of democracy in 1999, the Obasanjo administration has been successful in attracting additional investments totaling almost $13 billion since 2000.

The industry is dominated by the government-owned Nigerian National Petroleum Company (NNPC) and major foreign multinationals in the industry including American companies such as Chevron-Texaco, Exxon Mobil, French giant TotalFina Elf and the Anglo Dutch Shell oil company. The government engages all market players through Joint Venture Agreement (JVA) documents; which are legal contracts that govern the exploration and production of Nigeria's oil resources. Although there is much speculation about Nigeria's reserves as new reserves are constantly discovered as exploration continues in the deepwater regions, it is estimated that the country has a guaranteed output for the next 60 years.

What is assured is that the country will become the dominant gas producer in the region in the long term. Falling on the bad experiences of the oil industry, successive administrations are trying to get this one right. Investing $4 billion into the Nigerian Liquefied Natural Gas (NLNG) scheme, Africa's largest engineering project; gas is set to trump oil exports as Nigeria's main moneymaker by 2012. The main challenge the country faces though is curtailing the flagrant flaring of natural gas which has affected hundreds of fishing villages in the Niger Delta region. Of primal note is the degradation and neglect of the Niger-Delta which has created militant uprisings that often lead to kidnappings of foreign oil workers, who are usually released. The downstream sector of the oil industry is vibrant as private oil marketing companies distribute petroleum products, through a massive network system. Virtually all multinational oil firms are engaged in the lucrative marketing business and have listed their distribution subsidiaries on the NSE.

Telecommunications

Would you believe me if I told you that in 1960, with a population of 63 million, Nigeria only had 18,724 phone lines? Fast-forward to the year 2000, things must have improved surely you would think but once again, the answer is no. The country had an installed capacity of 700,000 lines but only 450,000 were active giving the country one of the lowest teledensity rates in the world. And mind you, these were landlines! Did you mention text messaging and voicemail? Forget about it! To remedy the embarrassing situation, the Obasanjo administration granted operating licenses to three cellular phone companies including the government-owned phone company, NITEL. By 2001, a well defined telecom policy that initiated a deregulated market was formulated and implemented to jumpstart competition amongst service providers.

Between 2002 and 2005, Nigeria had become the fastest telecom market in the world with an annual growth rate of 37% driven mainly by an explosion in mobile telephony. The telecoms sector is one of the miracles of economic reform in Nigeria as the country moved from only half a million telephone customers in 2000 to an estimated 18 million users in only three years. Massachusetts-based telecom research firm, Pyramid Research, forecasts the subscriber base to top 50 million and annual revenues of $7.3 billion for telecom providers by 2010. There has been some reluctance by some of the mobile phone companies to be listed on the stock exchange but it seems inevitable as they require massive sums to finance long-term expansion plans if they want to remain competitive as other telecom giants invade Nigeria.

RECENT DEVELOPMENTS & LONG TERM ISSUES

Now that you have a good understanding of Nigerian political and economic history to impress your friends with, it would be useful to picture where the country stands currently and the challenges to its long-term development plans. The political, industrial and infrastructural facets of the economy are primary concerns for long term investors.

Political and Regulatory environment

In Nigeria, political power is resident in the tripartite agencies of the Presidency, Legislature and Judiciary. The advent of democratic government in 1999, has allowed the Obasanjo administration strengthen democratic institutions and make serious efforts to stamp out corruption which is an endemic way of life in the country. However, sectarian violence in Northern Nigeria and youth militancy in the oil-rich Niger Delta region intermittently arise as major threats to the nascent democracy and the prospects of long term foreign direct investment in the country. The Nigerian judiciary is regarded as one of the best-trained in the world, with many of the country's leading jurists assigned by the Federal government to help build entire legal systems in smaller African countries. At home though, the judiciary has lost the appeal of most Nigerians (probably because it is so much harder to sue your boss than in the US) who are frustrated by the slow pace of judicial executions and sensational reports of corrupt judges manipulating cases for the right price.

In the past, successive Nigerian administrations have been dogged by policy inconsistencies and reversals. The situation has made long term investing impractical in sectors such as mining which need stable policies to support long term capital projects. For investors, priority should be accorded sectors where there exists defined regulatory oversight and infrastructure such as the banking, telecommunications, food services, capital market and energy sectors. Noteworthy is the fact that no matter the prevailing macro-economic and political situation in the country, the ultimate performance of your portfolio is based on your knowledge of the country and how much time you are willing to commit to studying how general news events influence your stockholdings.

Infrastructure

Power supply in the country is largely epileptic and requires huge capital investment to sustain the growing demand for electricity. The current situation causes a major expense for business owners and is a particular drain on small businesses' cash reserves. For medium to large-scale firms, the viable option is to seek power sharing arrangements by building gas distribution networks for their operations. The Federal Government in 2005 finalized the break up of the government power utility into 11 separate companies and is auctioning them off to qualified bidders. The once moribund telecom sector is relatively efficient although there are incidents of poor telecom services in the hinterland, a concern for companies involved in extractive industries such as mining and petroleum production in rural locations.

Overall, telecommunication service in major urban centers is sophisticated. The transportation network in Nigeria is fairly extensive but several major highways are dilapidated and require repairs almost on an annual basis. For companies engaged in moving goods to customers across the country, this is a major challenge. Some have opted to use the railway system which is very inexpensive and inefficient at the same time. The distribution of portable drinking water is a huge problem in many Nigerian cities as various tiers of government squabble over allocation of water resource funds. Thousands of Nigerian entrepreneurs have taken the opportunity to meet demand with the construction of private water purification facilities.

An excellent privatization scheme managed by the Bureau of Public Enterprises (BPE) is responsible for divesting government interests in enterprises that are best run by the private sector, and engaged in finding equity investors and technical partners to take over former government enterprises. The security situation in the country is less than optimum as police response time is low and corruption still exists in a substantial segment of security agencies. The situation is particularly difficult for multinational companies engaged in the oil business, located in southern Nigeria, who have to contend with kidnap scenarios and the prospect of oil facilities being vandalized by militant youth who feel disenfranchised from the billions of dollars that have been reaped but not reinvested in their communities. However, the security situation in Nigeria should be taken into context as robberies and other violent crimes have not escalated since 2002. In fact, major cities in the country such as Abuja, Kaduna and Port Harcourt are as safe as any large city in the United States.

Industry

Industrial capacity utilization currently stands at 52.7% with agriculture and manufacturing leading growth between 2002 and 2005. Overall, the business climate is a tough one for local industrialists who are plagued by high production costs as a result of petroleum price increases, higher tariffs on imported raw materials and the growing competition posed by the smuggling of cheap imports from Asia. Analysts estimate that the contribution of manufacturing to GDP is less than 6% and falling because of smuggling. Many entrepreneurs' expansion plans are constrained by inadequate funding from the banking sector but are seeking competitive local packages from the government owned Bank of Industry. On the bright side, Nigerian banks are aiding local industrialists source project financing from global fund managers and independent government agencies such as the US-based Overseas Private Investment Corporation (OPIC) that aids American firms invest abroad; particularly in emerging markets such as Nigeria. However, there are sectors that possess huge growth opportunity for any caliber of investor. Massive foreign investment is rising in key sectors such as:

- Power and Gas
- Real Estate

- Transportation
- Commodity Trading
- Services
- Food and Beverages
- Information Technology and Telecommunications
- Textile

Investing in Nigeria, no matter the sector is an exciting and often profitable experience for an informed investor. If you seek more information on the economy and society, visit your local library reference. For now, our focus is on the stock market and how you can profitably make money in this country. With the information provided, you have a better chance than others at taking that critical step of expanding your investment portfolio to include Nigerian companies. In the next chapter, I will introduce you to the fun stuff: the Nigerian financial industry and of course, the stock market.

Chapter 2
The Birth of Broad Street

One of the most sensational movies chronicling the high-stakes world of finance is the classic *Wall Street*, where a maverick super-investor (great sounding title don't you think?) schools an ambitious but naïve stockbroker in the cutthroat corporate takeover business, where smart businessmen buy faltering companies, reorganize their operations and then sell them for a much higher price, keeping a hefty profit. In a particular scene, the young broker returns to his office and it is total chaos as tens of brokers are on the phone calling investors and using every sales tactic to harangue a dollar out of them to buy stocks in companies; whether they be good or bad picks. Cold calling is the order of the day on these trading floors as brokers try to convince individuals who think they can make a quick buck off a 'hot tip' from someone who just thought it will be nice to help them out with a hot stock tip. Yeah right!

Fiction turns into reality as the same scene plays out daily on the many trading floors stretching from New York to London and Frankfurt. Watching stockbrokers brutally twist the minds of investors through incredulous and almost ridiculous sales pitches has been one of the most brutal experiences for me. Kind of reminds me of the movie *Boiler Room*. Okay, I have a fetish for movies with corporate intrigue themes but I can't help it! In comparison to the major financial markets, the Nigerian stock market can be called 'humane' as brokers are restricted to providing information to clients who request advice from them and unsolicited calls are banned at the moment. This allows brokers to focus on building relationships with their clients on a level more personable than what obtains on major global markets. The hype that is often the trigger for stock buying frenzies on major American trading floors is minimal and most trades for informed investors are conducted on the basis of fundamental analysis, a subject we will discuss in Chapter 5. The core of financial activity takes place on a two mile stretch of concrete and imposing glass buildings in the downtown section of Lagos Island. Welcome to Broad Street, home to one of the largest financial districts on the African continent. Just like the famed Wall Street, Broad Street houses an array of investment banks and brokerages that manage the investment portfolios and bank accounts of millions around the country and indeed, around the world. Although many financial service firms have moved to other parts of the city to ply their trade, Broad Street is really where it happens.

In the following pages, you will be privy to the origin of the Nigerian financial system and understand how the Nigerian stock market operates. This knowledge should provide a clear perception of the market and help prepare you to invest in Nigerian stocks.

HUMBLE BEGINNINGS

In 1890, a consortium of British banks namely Lloyds of London, National Provincial and Westminster; established an overseas office in Lagos. Called the African Banking Corporation or ABC, the bank primarily served the credit needs of British merchants in the region, quickly spreading to other parts of Africa and eventually taking over the banking operations of *Elder Dempster*, a shipping company that held a monopoly over West African maritime trade. In 1893, the consortium reviewed their operations in Africa, came to the verdict that full-fledged banking was not a profitable business in Africa and started shopping around for a buyer. Around this time, the original managers of Elder Dempster had formed a rival bank called the Bank of British West Africa (BBWA) which had cultivated stronger banking relations with British merchants and had started exploring the niche of wealthy and educated Nigerians who were wresting market share from the Britons and other Europeans in the lucrative commodity markets in the Northern and South Eastern regions.

In 1894, shipping magnate Alfred Jones who owned Elder Dempster successfully negotiated the repurchase of his former banking division for 12,000 British pounds and integrated it into the BBWA; making it the largest bank in the West African sub region. Over a century later, the small BBWA has changed its name to First Bank of Nigeria with a balance sheet size exceeding N510 billion ($4.2 billion) and millions of customers across the African continent. I am sure that descendants of the shareholders in the British consortium that sold ABC would be kicking themselves in the foot as the bank is reputed to have a long track record of increasing dividend payments!

From the early 1900s to the mid-twentieth century, the banking industry thrived as Nigerians returning from academic study and living in the United States and United Kingdom encouraged the local citizenry to use the banking system to empower themselves economically. However, most banking transactions took place at the corporate level as the public had the tendency to hold real cash in their hands, rather than place their faith in a piece of paper called a check. Sorry, I digress. It took some time for some structure to be put in place for the growing financial industry, but by 1952 an ordinance was passed requiring bank regulation, setting reserve fund levels and providing assistance for some emerging banks owned by Nigerians. In the same year, Nigerian members of the Federal House of Assembly proposed the formation of a central bank to facilitate formal economic development in the country.

The British members of the House, worried that this was a vital step in moving the country to political independence, led a defeat of the motion on the grounds that it was more important to have a capital market that will fund investments in the real sector of the economy. Following pressure from the Nigerian members, a study was commissioned in 1957 that eventually recommended the establishment of a central bank; particularly as calls for independence from England reached a crescendo. In March 1958, draft legislation was presented before the Nigerian parliament on the issue. The act was subsequently passed and by July 1, 1959; the Central Bank of Nigeria (CBN) came into full operation and started issuing the national currency.

GENTLEMEN, BEHOLD THE STOCK MARKET

As Nigeria struggled on the political stage to find a sound footing to satisfy its many nationalities, the financial industry trudged ahead with the backing of vital legislation and patriotic officials who implemented the fiscal policies of the government of the day. As capital funds built up in the nation's coffers and local bank reserves, the management of the CBN embarked on nurturing a workable capital and money market. The reasoning behind the bank's shift from fiscal and monetary policy implementation to building the Nigerian stock market was one of national pride and strategic interest, rather than real economic development. In the absence of a formal capital market, all savings and deposit balances were funneled through the banking system; with major capital balances being invested for the country abroad on the London Stock Exchange. This was unacceptable to the early managers of Nigeria's financial industry and they took steps to remedy the situation. The first step to a real stock market occurred in 1960 when the CBN issued treasury bills to finance the country's first development plans. Seeking an official platform for government agencies and private companies doing business in the greater Lagos area to source funds, the Lagos Stock Exchange (LSE) was formed in 1960 and became operational in 1961. With an annual subvention coming from the CBN, the LSE was incorporated under the companies' ordinance that gave it legal coverage as an association limited by guarantee and commenced trading with 19 listed securities. The independence provided the LSE from its very beginning has helped the Nigerian stock market maintain a strong autonomy from the political influence of successive administrations.

MARKET PERFORMANCE

Even during the darkest days of military rule in Nigeria, the market weathered the storm and its indices grew steadily even when investment in the real economy was declining. In 1977, the LSE changed its name to the Nigerian Stock Exchange (NSE) and has still continued trading operations from its Customs House office in downtown Lagos. Since then, trading floors have been opened across the country to service investors located faraway from Lagos. In 1984, when the NSE adopted a formal index now known as the NSE All-Share Index; it started at 100 basis points. In August 2006, the NSE All-Share index had climbed to 25021.24 listed 206 companies on its bourse, including 11 government stocks and 49 industrial loans with a total market capitalization of $30.1 billion and the market was ranked in the top 15 global performing markets. Despite calls for the introduction of sophisticated trading instruments that are the norm on major international stock markets, the NSE strictly trades securities, government and corporate bonds.

According to NSE estimates, there are over 4 million Nigerians investing in the market along with over 100 institutional investors. If you have never invested abroad, talk less of the Nigerian economy; maybe you would find comfort in the knowledge that 47% of the market is controlled by foreign investors; mainly British conglomerates and Nigerians living in the Diaspora. In 2005, it was estimated that Americans owned $450 million worth of shares in Nigerian companies. In 2003, the market capitalization of the NSE grew by a spectacular 70%, return on investments between 1997 and 2004 exceeded 233% and Federal Treasury bonds offered returns of 18%. In 2003, the NSE had one of the top five highest returns in the world, peaking at a 59% return in dollar terms. Global financial analysts will tell you that these statistics are among the highest in the world.

THE PRIMARY AND SECONDARY MARKETS

The NSE exists to provide long-term financing for Nigeria's growing economy, providing a mechanism to mobilize private and public savings that have created some of the largest businesses in Nigerian history. The NSE has structured company classification according to the first and second tier-markets. The first-tier market is where the larger corporations with longer tenure of operations and larger market capitalization are listed, while the second-tier segment which was created inn 1985 is home to smaller companies, usually those with capitalization less than $10 million. For academic purposes, let us understand two basic investment concepts that would help you time your trades; particularly when Nigerian companies seek investments from the public at the early stages of their business lives or when they need the money for a major business project.

In the **primary market**, companies who are listed or have never been listed on the Nigerian stock market can approach the NSE with a request to raise funds from the investing public. The mode of offer for such securities could be in the form of offer for subscription, right issues, private placements or sale offers. In the last fifteen years, there has been a significant change in trend as many hitherto private companies have piled into the market and raised substantial funds through Initial Public Offerings, popularly known as an IPO. How does an IPO work? Well, let us use a fictitious oil company called ABC Corporation which has been successful in the oil business for 30 years under the management of two brothers who work with the support of eleven staff members. Also the company reported revenues of $4.7 million in its last financial year and has a cash reserve of $800,000. Suddenly, geologists working for ABC discover an oil well that is guaranteed to hold 100 million barrels. Great news, don't you think? If they can successfully drill the oil and sell it, they would definitely make a lot of money. Hold on, just one big problem. The economist working for the company forecasts that drilling operations would cost ABC $12 million and help them realize their dreams of hitting pay dirt! While ABC's managers are scratching their heads on raising that unbelievable amount of money; Leke, the company's financial consultant suggests that they contact an investment bank to arrange an IPO. Once the investment bank meets with company management and discusses the financial issues that ABC faces and understands how the money will be put to use in the best interest of all parties, the investment bankers set to work; thumbing through thousands of documents, conducting market research to see if people like you and me would be interested in a company we have probably never heard about, and drafting important paperwork for presentation to the regulatory authorities for scrutiny.

After reviewing the IPO documentation, the chief regulator of the capital market, called the Securities and Exchange Commission (SEC) would determine if the deal is in the best interests of individual and institutional investors. If they consider that the company's proposal is in accordance with various Nigerian laws and investment acts; it approves the sale and the stocks are eventually presented to the public on the stock exchange. The investing public then buys the shares of the company listed, become part owners of a profitable business, ABC has the money to drill, drills and hits oil, sells oil and everyone becomes stinking rich! Well, not exactly but you get the picture.

A significant part of the total market capitalization of publicly listed companies in Nigeria was raised through IPOs between 1995 and 2005 and that growth pattern should hold steady under stable economic and political climates. With regard to prospective investors, the NSE and SEC have through new incentives eased the pain of foreign investors who were once restricted to marginal stakes in Nigerian companies. All companies listed on the NSE can initiate an IPO that foreign individuals and institutions can subscribe to without limits on their capital investments. In fact, Nigerian companies that meet certain requirements of the NSE can seek funds outside Nigerian shores through cross-border listings. One of the largest banks in Nigeria, the United Bank for Africa, is listed on the New York Stock Exchange where its shares can be purchased with American Depository Receipt (ADR) instruments.

Right now, you are probably thinking: "Hey, supposing I didn't hear about the IPO, that must be another missed opportunity". Do not despair my dear friend. This is where the **secondary market** comes to your rescue. The secondary market refers to the process of trading in shares that have already been issued in an initial private or public offering. So using our example, you can still call your broker and place an order to buy ABC shares once the IPO is over. Don't worry. The price could be the same, lower or higher; depending on how the overall market prices the stock. It all boils to timing and how you can make money from effectively timing your trade. Theorists argue over which market is more meaningful to engage in. What is agreed across both sides of the aisle is that the secondary market is the most dynamic for the investing public. Unlike the primary market where most of the wheel dealing is done in boardrooms and only God knows what other hideous place; the secondary market is the playground for investors and speculators. You might be one or the other or even better both! In Chapter 6, we will examine what kind of investor you are and how to discuss those goals with your broker so that your trades are in tandem with your overall investment objectives.

Knowing that corporate raiders will always try to monopolize stock ownership in certain companies, the NSE limits the nominal transfers of stock between family members and allied corporations who trade large amounts of stocks. In Nigeria, if you own 5% or more equity capital in a publicly quoted company, you are mandated by law to disclose your holdings to the NSE and SEC. If a corporation, there must be full disclosure of the stock interests of all company directors. So if you are making a lot of money in the Nigerian market and realize that your stock holdings have reached or exceeded the 5% limit (by God, you must be very rich by then!), contact your broker to aid you in filing the statutory documents to be in good stead with the government- you want to make money not get charged for a flimsy issue such as not filing a simple document.

On the NSE, initial listing of primary market stocks can be done in either the first or second tier markets, provided certain regulatory and business requirements are met. For the typical investor residing in the United States or Canada, investing in companies with market caps less than $50 million is considered risky in comparison to investing in the stock of giant companies such as General Electric, Microsoft or Boeing Aviation which boost market caps running in tens and even hundreds of billions of dollars.

In Nigeria, most of the first-tier companies have market caps running between $60 million and $5 billion but are considered large caps by local standards. It does not mean that they are not viable investments you should consider, it simply means that they should be viewed in a different context. All companies listed on the first-tier segment of the NSE must have operated profitably for five years preceding filing an application to regulators for listing on the exchange. For such companies to remain on the first-tier board, a minimum 25% of their outstanding shares should be in the hands of public investors at any point in time. Second-tier companies in Nigeria are very small by international standards, so small that very few Nigerians invest in them and as such; trading volumes are low and many investors in those companies complain of not receiving dividends in years. Listing requirements for such companies demand proof of profitable operations three years prior to the listing on the NSE and a minimum 10% of outstanding stocks should be held by the investing public. Investing in these companies should not be a first priority for investors who just seek to make money from trading stocks. However, if you review the companies traded and see a second-tier stock you like; contact a local financial advisor or stockbroker in Nigeria and discuss the viability of investing in that category of companies.

MARKET OPERATIONS

All transactions on the NSE are executed through an Automated Trading System (ATS), an electronic order book that matches the buy and sell orders of market participants in real time. The NSE opens for trading at 10:00am and closes 12:00pm daily at which time daily trade statistics are compiled and distributed around the world. If you have access to Reuters' International Network, you can look up the numbers for the NSE under the code NSXA-B. The exchange publishes these results daily, weekly, monthly, quarterly and annually. Starting in 2004, the NSE launched a remote online trading portal for stockbrokers around the world to access its trading engine, while making it much convenient for financial professionals to get market information to their clients on time.

With the ATS mechanism, market transactions are concluded within three working days (T+3). The NSE also has a Trade Guaranty Fund to manage the trades of brokers who have exceeded their trading limits. There is a major push by the major brokerages operating in the country and licensed foreign brokers to extend trading hours to accommodate the different time zones and expand the trading time for investors around the world. However, it would help you to know that the NSE has one of the most sophisticated technology platforms for trading in Africa, rivaling those of the larger Johannesburg (South Africa) and Cairo (Egypt) stock exchanges. To make sure fraudulent brokers do not try one of those mastermind online trading scams that prevailed in the US in the mid-1990s, the Securities and Exchange Commission uses online market surveillance software to monitor broker trades on the Abuja and Lagos floors of the NSE.

Now you do know that the market and brokers are going to get their cut, don't you? Thought you could escape that one? Ah....not so fast! It is easy to feel that trading costs are pricey (throw in the cost of transferring money to your trading account in Nigeria and the costs go up some more) and they sometimes are, but that is simply the cost of doing business. If you do not feel you have to pay anything to get something, either you are on the wrong planet or I need to move to your country (wherever that is) and celebrate *Free Fridays* with you all year long! Let us take a look at how your pocket gets pinched on the NSE; it happens everywhere, so don't fret. Focus on trading intelligently enough to make a profit that adequately covers the charges. Compared to the global markets, fees and levies on the NSE look prohibitive. Yes, you make all this good money but at the same time, you might bite your lips thinking of the extra change the market players are going to keep. I have a breakdown below for you to capture where it all goes.

FEE STRUCTURE

In Nigeria, the SEC is responsible for setting brokerage commissions using a sliding scale to determine transaction costs per trade, which could vary based on the amount of money you want to invest. From the fee schedule presented, you will see that the more you invest; the lower your transaction costs.

TRADE EXECUTION	FEE
Brokerage Commission (Buy and Sell Orders)	
On the first N500, 000 of consideration	2.75%
On the next N500, 000 of consideration	2.25%
On the next N2, 000,000 of consideration	2.00%
On the next N2, 000,000 of consideration	1.50%
Amounts over N5, 000,000 of consideration	1.00%
SEC Levy (Buy orders only)	1.00%
NSE Levy (Sell orders only)	0.25%
Contract Stamp (Buy and Sell Orders)	0.075%
CSCS Fee	0.10%
Value Added Tax (VAT)	0.1375%*

TRANSACTION SERVICES	FEE
Account Opening Fees	Nil
Monthly CSCS Account Statement	Nil
Money Transfer (In and out of Trading Account)	Nil
Transfer of Securities	Nil
Document Custodial services	Nil

*The VAT is a variable figure as it is normally calculated at 5% of the commission fee charged by your broker, which is then based on the amount of money you invest.

If we do some rough math, your transaction costs per trade could range anywhere from as low as 2.3% of your total trade when buying stock to as high as 3.85% when selling them. On the NSE, dealing members can help you buy and sell quoted securities under NSE rules and regulations; regardless of your nationality. This accentuates the fact that you should get a broker who has some experience working with international clients, particularly those that live in North America and Europe. The pricelist above is not static due to the fact some brokers may charge fees for some services. I personally am not a big fan of brokerages that charge so-called "administration fees". When shopping for a broker, ask them if they charge such fees; if they do, move on. There are others that offer the same or better service without such fees.

In the past, investors had problems managing the share certificates that came with buying or selling stocks on the NSE. People were losing them, spending too much time retrieving the same documents from the NSE and transferring shares to third parties was a hassle. In 1989, the NSE adopted the recommendations of the Federation of International Stock Exchanges to improve its clearing and settlement systems. In 1992, the prayers of frustrated investors were answered when the NSE in conjunction with private individuals, investment banks and stock broking firms formed a subsidiary company called the Central Securities Clearing System Limited (CSCS). This company was a Godsend. Trust me, I remember trying to transfer share certificates for a private client in Nigeria and it was the hardest thing next to dating the most beautiful girl in high school! The main function of the CSCS is to provide an integrated depository to sort out the messy details of a typical stock market transaction. If you are used to the sophisticated clearing systems of major stock exchanges like the NYSE or the Japanese Nikkei, this would sound very strange to you but for domestic and foreign investors at the time, it was a frustrating experience.

If you live outside Nigeria, there are many advantages to using the services of the CSCS. This includes access to free quarterly stock statements (you can get them on-demand for a $1 if you cannot wait), receipt of your share certificate and not worry about losing them because the CSCS has them stored electronically, and using your stock statements as collateral to obtain loans from Nigerian banks. In the event that you seek to transfer money in and out of Nigeria for the purpose of stock trading, the bank custodian that facilitates such transfers on behalf of local brokers would charge you a minimal fee. When shopping for a stockbroker in Nigeria, make it clear that you would like to know how much a typical trade will cost you and if there are additional cost-savings incentives they provide for new clients. In Chapter 6, I will show you how to select a good broker and explain why the operating environment is vital to your choice.

MARKET PARTICIPANTS

In the world of finance, it is simply amazing the number of people that work to facilitate a simple transaction like buying a burger, selling a stock, getting the best deal on a credit card and other scenarios. Let us look at the people that run the show in the Nigerian stock market.

Fund providers

As the Nigerian stock market has performed tremendously well on an index basis since its inception, it has attracted interest from the investing community. The major investors on the NSE are institutional investors comprised of mutual funds, pension funds and insurance companies. With the Nigerian legislature passing the revised Pension Reform Act of 2004, major investors such as the insurance firms, investment banks and discount houses started forming separate pension fund divisions. The act establishes a uniform and contributory private-sector managed and fully funded pension system for both the public and private sectors of the economy. This consolidation has contributed more money to the market than ever before. With large amounts of cash available to them, these managers hold significant stakes in Nigerian stocks and are market makers (firms that accept the risk of holding a large number of stock in a company facilitate strategic trading in that stock) in many stocks in the matured industries such as the banking, petroleum and food sectors on the NSE. Currently, pension fund administration in Nigeria is a $2.5 billion industry.

You might feel a little insignificant with just a couple thousands of dollars but do not despair my friend. There are an estimated 5 million Nigerians (including a growing number living outside the country) investing in the market and close to 80,000 individual foreign investors active in the market. Unlike the US, where over half of American households have funds invested in the stock market; independent economic analysts calculate that less than 4% of the Nigerian population could be classified as stock investors. Low income levels and a lack of investor education resources are cited as possible reasons for such low interest amongst the Nigerian public. However, interest in the market has gained momentum amongst young professional Nigerians, particularly amongst those in the 24-38 age brackets and although they have low pools of investable funds; their small contributions in the interim could shore up stock prices in the long run.

Publicly Traded Companies

I once thought of incorporating myself and getting an investment bank to do an IPO for me! Gosh, if only that was possible don't you think? Sorry, the stock market is not fantasy land, at least the last time I checked. After gathering your funds along with other fund providers, all the money collected goes to either private corporations or the government. Before you scream "Bloody Murder" because the government already takes money from you in the form of taxes and wants some more, let me break it down for you. The Nigerian government usually issues long-term financial instruments such as government bonds and treasury bills to finance many projects in the country such as the building of hospitals, roads and other infrastructure. In fact, the government has been doing this way before the creation of the NSE when the first recorded government bond worth 300,000 pound sterling government was issued in 1946; proceeds which were spent on various development projects. Ever since, successive political administrations have issued variants of the Federal Government Development Stocks. Treasury bills and certificates in Nigeria are relatively popular due to the high rates of return in comparison to what obtains on other international bond markets.

Major corporations also approach the market to finance growth in their respective sectors. Many companies go to their bankers for loans but there seems a significant benefit when they issue stock for you and me to buy. First of all they tend to keep our funds permanently (although we can retrieve our personal stakes when we sell our own portion of the business in the secondary market) and do not have to worry about deadlines and interest payments to banks. Secondly, no collateral is required to raise funds from the public. The only thing companies give up is equity in the business which is what you are gunning for. Private corporations dominate the NSE and there is no shortage of quality companies for you to invest in.

Financial Intermediaries

For every IPO or deal making that involves a publicly traded company, there are always teams of professionals working behind the scenes. It is essential that you know all about these professionals and the organizations they work for, if you must become the savvy investor in Nigerian stocks that you wish to be. Okay, let's meet your new friends in the game of investing.

Stockbrokers

The brokerage industry in Nigeria is past its infancy stage and has all the characteristics of established brokerages around the world except for the unnerving fact that a majority of the firms in the business lack the customer-service orientation that is taken for granted in the United States, Europe and some parts of Latin America. However, there are still a number of brokerages that are world-class; charging premium price for their services in the country (which should be very affordable to foreign investors) and execute trades more efficiently than others. Many of them have a lot of experience managing clients who live abroad, so you should be comfortable working with them. This is not an endorsement of their services but from my experience in the stock market, they would make investing in Nigeria as painless as possible for you. You can find a list of reputable brokers in the appendix section. In Chapter 6, we will look at how you should go about selecting a broker to execute your trades. Most brokerages in Nigeria conduct full-service operations and have investment professionals who can advise you on other opportunities such as foreign exchange trading, real estate management and investments in the oil and gas sector.

Investment Banks

Investment banking is one of the fastest growing sectors of the financial services industry in the country, particularly as local companies rush to raise funds from the public to take advantage of the industrial policies and fiscal incentives created under the Obasanjo administration. The universal banking system in the country has allowed these banks that were exclusively restricted to the merchant side of banking to engage in a variety of services including retail banking, lending, trade financing, trusteeship, wealth management and financial advisory services. Many investment banks are located in major cities across the country, building relationships with local investors so they can purchase the stock issued through the IPO deals they conduct on behalf of companies seeking listing on the NSE. Most investment banks operating in the country have correspondent agreements with major banks in the United States.

Company Registrars

Registrars are companies or individuals that are responsible for keeping records of investors' bonds and stock holdings. Their primary task is ensuring that the amount of shares outstanding matches the amount of shares issued and authorized by the company. Other things registrars do include registering share transfers, issuing those you lost or your dog ate!, distributing annual reports to existing and prospective investors, verification of shareholders' signatures on documents, organizing annual general meetings and liaising with the CSCS to update the shareholder register; particularly if you transfer shares to someone else.

Auditing firms

Auditing firms are companies that provide unbiased examination and evaluation of a company's financial statements. International auditing firms such as KPMG, Pricewaterhouse Coopers and other local accounting firms handle the bulk of auditing Nigeria companies. These firms go to the companies before they produce those glossy brochures and annual reports that they send to us, check the financial records of the company and report whether the company accurately stated or misrepresented the facts of their true financial condition.

It is a tough balancing act for these audit firms since they are normally appointed by the companies they audit in the first place! You might wonder how they maintain their neutrality in the process since they receive their compensation from the very company that selected them (usually through a competitive process, since the SEC does not force companies to choose specific audit firms). I guess the audit firms have to act on the neutrality and professionalism that their practice requires of them and is supposedly guaranteed to satisfy public trust. If you remember the Enron case where millions of Americans lost billions of dollars (many lost their retirement savings) to the financial mismanagement of the company by Enron executives, the growing problems that the company was facing up till it declared chapter 11 bankruptcy in December 2001 would have been discovered if not for the culpability of the company's auditors, Arthur Andersen. Arthur Andersen violated the trust of the investing public by assisting Enron 'cook the books' (using creative accounting to hide losses and present the image of a financially sound company) and eventually create the largest bankruptcy in American history. Today, the company has lost virtually all its clients and the prospects of the once respected audit firm returning to being a viable business is nil.

The price to be paid for falsehood is too high for such practices in Nigeria; since the Nigerian financial authorities are renowned for shutting down repeat offenders in the industry without warning. All public auditors are certified by the Institute of Chartered Accountants (ICAN) before they can practice audit functions in the country. A cautionary note to foreign investors: do not invest in any Nigerian company that does not have an audited report from qualified auditors operating in the country. If you are skeptical about the authenticity of an auditor's report in an annual report, contact the auditing firm directly for confirmation. Better safe than sorry.

REGULATORS

In 1994, the Central Bank of Nigeria formed a central body consisting of key members of the financial industry to bring some formal regulatory oversight over the Nigerian financial industry. Before then, it was a hassle getting approval for companies seeking to go public. Teams of corporate lawyers, stockbrokers, financial advisors and everyone else that mattered had to hop from one government department to the other; wasting valuable time and giving ample room for mischievous insider trading to go on. Accorded legal status by the 1998 amendment to Section 38 of the CBN Act of 1991, the agency was called the Financial Services Regulation Coordinating Committee (FSRCC) and is in charge of supervising activity in the nation's financial markets. Members of the FSRCC include the CBN, SEC, the Federal Ministry of Finance, Corporate Affairs Commission and the National Insurance Commission.

The main agency that monitors the capital market is the Securities and Exchange Commission (SEC). This is the watchdog (some operators call it the bulldog) that monitors the NSE and ensures that companies presented to the investing public are worthy of listing. Apart from its regulatory and investigation responsibilities, the SEC authorizes the establishment of unit trusts and mutual funds and scrutinizes any government bonds that the CBN might bring to the market on behalf of Federal and State governments. In 1990, the SEC initiated a consultative and advisory body called the Capital Market Committee to serve as a forum for representatives of the commission and market operators to deliberate on issues that affect the capital market and suggest ways for improving its operations. The Nigerian Stock Exchange is a self-regulated entity, operating without government intervention of any sort and owned and managed by private sector participants.

Chapter 3
The Nigerian Stock Market

In the late nineties, my family relocated from Northern Nigeria to the largest and craziest city in Nigeria, Lagos. With 16 million people jostling with me to suck up any form of oxygen in this coastal city; I still wonder why we made that move. However, I am grateful for the move because Lagos was where I had my first lesson in the stock market. Visiting downtown Lagos to shop with my mother, I was so overwhelmed with the serious look on the face of the men and women, dressed impeccably, walking into the surrounding skyscrapers on Broad Street. Late at night, while my siblings dozed off as 9 O'clock news channel came on, I was wide awake waiting for my favorite news segment. The one where some guy would ramble off some numbers, talking about indexes, share depreciation, bull this and bear that. It was all confusing but at the same time, intriguing. I was totally transfixed by the video footage in the background of men moving up and down on the floor screaming like mad dogs, waving pieces of paper and looking at screens that had very grotesque symbols and numbers rolling off.

Watching the chaos, my dad would call them a 'pack of gamblers'. All I saw was crazy men making serious cash. The conflicting views of father and son are still repeated today amongst many investors. And the reason why there is so much mystery about stock investing is that many people do not understand how financial markets work, who is involved in and how they can profit from stock investing. This chapter is focused on unveiling that mystery by showing you how and why stocks exist.

If you are an experienced investor, you can skip this chapter. If not, it would be a great help to you. Let me make this clear: the most dangerous stock investor is one who focuses on the stock and does not understand the underlying issues that govern how that stock works. Stocks are mere financial tools, representing real companies that produce real goods and services for consumers. Stocks are ordinary financial vehicles that could lead to your financial freedom only if you understand how they work, how to use information and how to get in at the right time. As you well know, the prices of stocks go up and down; so do many other things including the sun and sometimes your personal moods. The key to success is being able to manage the cycles in a manner that keeps you on top most of the time and puts money in your pocket. As global markets become integrated and economic uncertainty affects how you view investing abroad and at home, it becomes essential that you have specific information on the economies you want to invest in; and not rely on the generic investing books that tell you how to invest in general. Before you put money on the table, let us go back and see how Nigerian companies are using the gift of an IPO to take advantage of business opportunities in Africa's largest economy.

NIGERIAN COMPANIES KNOCKING ON DOORS

For a long time, Nigerian companies have been out of luck in raising money to finance their operations. Interest rates on domestic loans are high and so prohibitive that many promising companies have collapsed under the weight of interest payments; if you have ever been in debt like I have in the past, you know how debilitating it could be- now multiply that by a thousand times and you probably would beg your smart friend not to do the math for you! So what they did they do? They headed abroad to seek financing from major banks in Europe. Most were lucky sourcing financing from British banks because of the cultural and economic ties between both countries but unfortunately, the negative image that the outside world had about Nigeria simply broke the camels back for many of them. Great business ideas, skilled staff and no money meant no business. However, the Nigerian stock exchange has become one of the most viable options for companies in the country, including multinational firms who seek significant funds to finance critical purposes such as financing research and development, increasing production capacity, technology upgrades, paying off debt or taking advantage of a business opportunity in its industry.

Luckily for investors, the NSE has a majority pool of companies that have track records of successful management and stable revenue earnings. Unlike the NYSE where many companies started just a few months ago, with no financial track record can rake in millions of dollars through an IPO, the NSE has relatively stringent rules for prospective listed companies with a focus on steady earnings and profitability over the preceding five years. In all fairness, it is true that some companies that have approached the market that way in the US have gone on and become multibillion dollar companies with strong balance sheets and active participants in the economy. However, millions of Americans will never forget the disastrous Internet bubble of the 1990s where billions of dollars were invested and lost in companies that had little more than a phone and desk as corporate headquarters, a hastily written business plan, twenty-something year olds with little or no business experience as CEOs and the hype of flawed financial analysts on Wall Street.

For now, hype is a small factor in determining how Nigerians buy domestic stocks as the fundamentals are hammered out above road shows and fast-talking brokers. Investing in Nigerian companies listed on the first-tier of the market means investing in solid companies with great financials. Some of the up comers that raise money through an IPO usually have strong brand recognition within Nigeria and could be excellent investment options. Contact a broker for advice on companies that are approaching the market for the first time. Make sure those first-timers have been in business for at least three years and have earnings growth exceeding 15% over the same period.

THE ART OF THE I.P.O.

Between 1995 and 2005, Broad Street experienced its highest level of mergers and acquisitions activity, public offerings and market cap growth. The reason for the flurry of activity is easy to grasp: the economy was opening up and key sectors were expanding rapidly, needing strong companies that had the resources to take advantage of the opportunity. As such, many firms approached the market through initial public offerings. It is no surprise that the market capitalization of the NSE has climbed by over 900% in the same period. Without a doubt, the IPO is the golden gate to investing in the Nigerian stock market. By simply contacting a stockbroker in Nigeria, you can have access to the latest IPOs that you could take advantage of.

The truth about an IPO is that any investor can make money in companies that issue them, whether they are in bull or bear markets. In bull markets, prices of such companies rise outrageously high in the first days of trading, allowing you make some cool change for getting in immediately the offer is open for subscription. In bear markets, companies will try to attract investors by discounting their stock prices to a level that most investors can afford. If the company has great potential, a solid business plan and innovative managers; the price usually picks up fairly soon. With the Nigerian stock market, the question you are dying to ask is, "how do I get in early"? Well, it is not that easy for individual investors because the investment banks and brokerage firms usually involved in the underwriting of a company's shares normally take sizable chunks of stock before they sell what they have to first, their clients and then, other investors. What is the moral of that insight? Get a broker who does a lot of investment banking deals and is kind enough to call you when such an opportunity pops up.

However, let me say this: be very careful when it comes to buying a stock through an IPO. Many IPOs are over-hyped and may be the work of unscrupulous brokers trying to sell a piece of crap called a company. In such circumstances, stick to your instincts and follow these tips: research the company, check out all the news you can find on the planned IPO, ignore your broker if he is all puffed up about the stock but cannot give you tangible reasons for investing in the company and be patient- never rush.

Nigerian companies are using the IPO and traditional means to build the economy and create wealth for investors who are willing to partake in the greatest stock market revolution in Africa. Let's look at 5 reasons why you might be interested in investing in this foreign country.

5 REASONS WHY YOU SHOULD INVEST IN NIGERIAN COMPANIES

Of all the sections in this book, this might be the page you ACTUALLY feel like reading! For most Nigerians and those who have done business in any African country, there might be a lesser need to justify why your investment portfolio should contain Nigerian stocks. I want you to know that it is not my intention to "convince" you or "sell" you on investing in Nigeria. If you are not remotely considering the possibility or have strong reservations towards investing on the NSE, I strongly urge you not to make serious plans to contact a Nigerian stockbroker. With limited access to Pan-African research, this book eliminates the main problem millions of investors face when trying to figure out how to invest in Nigerian and other African capital markets: lack of reliable and factual information. Be assured that this book would not answer all the questions you have (there are tons of resources online and at your local library that will shape your investment thought process about Nigeria). But for those of you who need 5 reasons to validate your investment horoscope (it sounds cheesy, but every book seems to scream 7 this or 10 that, I had to pick a number and I like 5!), here they are.

#1 FAST GROWING ECONOMY, FASTER GROWING STOCKS

The NSE is located in the largest economy in Africa which has the human and natural resources to break into the big league nations in the next 30 years. With a population of 138 million growing at an annual rate of 2.4%, Nigeria is the largest market for goods and services on the continent; attracting multibillion dollar investments in critical industries that are serving the basic needs of the people. Democracy has taken hold in a country once regarded as a pariah nation and investors from all over the world are for the first time in a long time (with the aid of real-time world and financial news) becoming aware of the country's potential and are steadily committing funds to projects that have surprised them with guaranteed returns. Something only few foreigners, particularly from Europe, Asia and South Africa have known for some time.

As publicly traded companies in Nigeria raise funds, they are investing that money in projects that have been thirsting for investments. Remember, the telecom example mentioned earlier? In 2000, getting a telephone in Nigeria was a luxury and many foreign firms were scared to invest in Nigeria; considering the country's negative past. A South African company, MTN communications took the risk of entering a market that global investment analysts had called an "investor's nightmare" and invested $1.4 billion in 2002. By the end of 2005, MTN Nigeria had a subscriber base of 8.6 million cell phone users, revenues of

$1.3 billion and profits of $330.3 million. The figures may be amazing but think of the fact that there is still room for expansion as less than 27% of the market has been tapped. Before this book went to press, a publicly listed MTN Nigeria was on the block and in talks with regulators. Telecom is just one of many sectors that local companies are desperate to take advantage of.

#2 CHEAP IS GREAT!

Quick quiz! Can you remember the awesome stock movement of the world's largest search engine Google.com? No? Okay, it goes like this. August 19, 2004 the company launches an anticipated IPO at $85 per share. Share price closes at $100.34 at day's end. On January 11, 2006; Google was trading at $471.63 a share. Makes you want to cry for not having a mere $85,000 (two years salary for an entry-level computer programmer in Idaho by the way) to buy a miserly 1000 units of the stock. Let's get realistic. If you don't have the money to buy expensively priced shares and don't have the heart to rob a bank to finance your financial dreams, the way to go is penny stocks. Penny stocks? Yes, down and dirty cheap stocks. The Nigerian stock market offers you the best priced deals you could ever get with the dollar. For example, as at June 19, 2006; the most expensive stock on the NSE was Mobil Nigeria valued at N160, the equivalent of $1.30 per share. With healthy price-earnings ratios, Nigerian companies are delivering world class returns on investment. The point being made is that you don't have to break the bank to become a serious investor in Nigeria. In 2001, I bought shares in a little-known bank called Access Bank for N1.00 (less than a cent) per share and gained a 317% return in 14 months. A $10,000 investment in an American stock may not register a blip in the investment community's radar but the same amount positions you to make profitable trades in the Nigerian stock market, at your discretion, market timing working in your favor and a little research (more on research in Chapter 5). So save yourself the trouble of expensive stocks on the major world markets. Buy small and win big!

#3 LOW CORRELATIONS WITH MAJOR WORLD MARKETS

There is a strange but logical thing that occurs in major financial markets:

the power of news and how it spreads across the world. Let's step back to the late 1990s, when the Asian and Russian stock markets tanked and how the world's economy caught the flu in a hard beat. It makes you wonder, "Why in the world does something that occurs in another country whose name I cannot even pronounce affect my investment back home"? Simple questions, simple answer. As globalization takes over, the major markets are all linked together in some strange way with brokers on both sides of the globe seeking to make money both ways, flattening arbitrage opportunities.

In the process, African economies have been sidelined due to low trade and consumption levels; allowing smart investors (of which you are about to become one) take advantage of an insulated Nigerian stock market. If you are seeking to diversify your portfolio in emerging markets' equities and still minimize volatility, investing in Nigerian stocks could be an excellent investment option. From a currency risk perspective, you will gain significantly by investing on the NSE as stock prices of listed companies have outperformed currency risk over the years; guaranteeing returns over managed money funds.

#4 OIL AND GAS: RUNNING ON FULL

Nigeria is the largest oil and third largest gas producer in Africa and with energy prices rising at astronomical levels in the late 1990s and showing no sign of slowing down in the early 21st century, the country has racked up such a huge foreign reserve that it had to enlist the expertise of global investment banks such as JP Morgan, HSBC and UBS to join local banks in managing it. From a negative balance in 2000, the country had over $32 billion in foreign reserve accounts by mid 2006 that the government has positioned to finance long-term development plans. Under a more transparent economic regime, those funds would be committed to developing Nigeria's inadequate infrastructure which would free companies to build their core businesses rather accruing huge costs that eat into their profits.

As gas easily replaces oil as the leading revenue earner and with telecoms catching up fast, the country should be awash in some serious cash by 2009 that will spur huge investments in the market. As incomes rise and more Nigerians invest in the market (domestic stock market participation grew by 30% between

1990 and 2005), a market boom in Nigerian equities is inevitable. Unlike in many 'developed' economies including major oil producers such as Saudi Arabia which have well developed downstream oil sectors, the local oil industry is largely untapped and provides huge opportunities for industrial and marketing expansion. Many of the companies that would lead the drive for expanding distribution and exploration projects in the gas sector are listed on the NSE, making them excellent investment vehicles for investors that seek opportunity in companies that provide a service that without a doubt will be in demand for years to come.

#5 PRIVATIZATION

Over the years, government-owned corporations have performed below par and have been symbols of corruption and financial mismanagement. From the mid-1990s to the current democratic dispensation, the Nigerian government has actively implemented an aggressive privatization policy to minimize government involvement in business. This move has been applauded by local economists who claim that government has no business in business. With multibillion dollar state-owned companies in the telecom, energy, aviation, insurance, sugar, banking and agriculture sectors set to hit the auction market; you have the opportunity of partaking in a major financial revolution in Nigeria that would put serious money in your pocket.

If you don't understand why privatization is a good reason for you to contemplate investing in Nigeria, allow me refresh your memory with what happened in Russia after the fall of communism. With a falling ruble, the Russian federation could not sustain its former state-owned monopolies and opened them up to private investors. As cash flowed into these companies through private placements and public issues on the Moscow Stock Exchange; management and financial dealings became more transparent and created room for efficiency. In the process, productivity increased and those companies with a healthy dose of investment funds maintained stable earnings. Nigeria has always been a step ahead of the game as previous administrations had in many instances, maintained majority stakes (usually 51%) in these corporations and allowed private managers do the real work. With total government divestment in many industries, the path to efficient and profitable companies being listed on the NSE is clear. Investors who get in now would be the pioneer reapers of the anticipated windfall in the Nigerian stock market.

With the market growing in bounds and leaps, it might make sense for you to research the full nature of this market and see if you can create wealth for yourself in a niche economy. You might find more than 5 reasons to invest in the Nigerian stock market; hopefully they would be seven-digit reasons!

FINDING YOUR INVESTMENT STYLE

If you have watched the trading floor of any stock exchange, you may come to the conclusion that all stock investors must have a love affair with noise and chaos and are silently praying for a heart-attack to hit them while they make a fast buck! Yes, the stock market can be a very exciting environment that gets the blood going but truth be told that there are a variety of emotions going on at any given time. There are Jim Cramer-type investors who thrive on bullishness and speculative opportunities and in the other corner, there are calm and collected investors that watch the market and have a simple steady plan that guides their investment style. Both types of investors can and do make money. The issue then is deciphering what kind you are. Before you invade the Nigerian stock market with your investment dollars, this is one of the biggest issues you have to consider. This is purely a psychological exercise that would set the precedent for your investment style in the future.

Your investment style has to be consistent and more importantly, profitable or at the very least capable of preserving your initial investment. A haphazard attitude to investing is dangerous not only while investing in stocks but with relation to your entire financial health. Your moods may change, you are human; but your investment style should not. The Nigerian market is not really hype-driven (at least for now, let's wait for the speculative vultures to arrive!) and tends to favor the long term investor, although major market makers or investors with deep pockets could spark off speculative trading in specific stocks. As you forge your investment strategy, certain factors would influence your investment strategy and financial experts sometimes differ on what should influence your investing style. I will touch on three that I feel are relevant as you proceed in your investing journey.

RISK TOLERANCE

Risk is the presence of uncertainty in an uncertain world. Gosh, that sounds so cheesy; so let me rephrase it with something more financial sounding. Risk is the probability that the actual result of an event would be different from the expected one. In the stock market, there is always the presence of risk. As I stated earlier and I will repeat it again, the stock market could be a very volatile environment with stock prices going up and down. Price movements are the result of many factors; including the mystery "X factor" that includes the unknown. The golden rule about risk in the stock market is pretty simple: "More risk, greater return; less risk, lower returns". While researching for this book, I had some people ask me, "If I invest my money in the Nigerian stock market, would you help me double it within 12 months for sure without losing any of it"? An innocent question it appears but unrealistic. I have personally experienced a 300% return on a stock investment in a leading Nigerian bank within 15 months. Does that qualify me to state that there is no risk in the market? No.

Some people chicken out at the thought of losing a dime while others could be very aggressive investors. If you are a cautious investor who prefers the realm of guaranteed security (by the way, there is no such thing); you can find safety in government bonds as many do and invest in a number of income stocks that have a consistent growth and earnings pattern. There is nothing wrong with having a low tolerance for risk and trust me, if you have a consistent investment pattern and work with an advisor that suggests quality fixed-income securities and stocks, you can still make a lot of money. On the other hand, if you are a daredevil investor who just loves the dynamism of the stock market and have the funds to conduct trades at will; your capacity for risk is much higher and could position your portfolio for huge gains. However, if the tide turns against you; you could get your fingers badly burnt. In Chapter 7, we will take a detailed look at risk, not just the theoretical definitions but how it affects your investment in Nigeria and how you can protect yourself. As you will see, risk in Nigeria could be very different from risk in the United States.

AGE

As you struggle to find your identity in the investment world, something that you should take into consideration is your age. Yes, that big ole' two or three digit number that seems to go up every year to your chagrin and your friends never let you forget! There seems to be so much stereotyping when it comes to comparing the investment habits of older and younger people; although there are distinct differences in how both groups approach investing in general.

Research shows that a majority of the aggressive investors in global stock markets are young people, normally between the ages of twenty-four and thirty-nine. At the beginning phase of the investor cycle, they have an unquenchable thirst for risk and are more receptive to stocks in new and untested industries. The fear of financial doom is lesser amongst younger investors as their youth and relative better health conditions allow them get back on their feet if and when they take a hit. If you fall within this age group, you might find yourself working longer hours and most likely two or more jobs to raise the money to start a family, buy a home or finance a graduate education. Although most investments of this group are in growth stocks, many in the sub-age bracket of 29-35 are actively looking at the safer refuge of bonds as they start planning for retirement early in their working lives.

Your investment style if you are over 45 would tend to be more conservative as you seek to preserve your wealth for retirement and to pass something on to your heirs. Most of the older crowd has a more balanced investment portfolio with funds usually spread into real estate, bonds and a smaller portion in stocks. After working hard to reach where you are (pay mortgage, send kids to college and splurge on that plasma TV your spouse was totally against!), you are not about to lose it all in the stock market. As I said, the stereotypes abound as I know a gentleman well into his sixties that has most of his funds in stocks and he is making a killing. No matter how old (or young) you are, make sure that your investment style is in sync with your ultimate financial goals.

INCOME LEVEL

How much you earn and what your potential earning power stands at is a huge determinant of your investing style. When writing this book I kept asking myself how much a person should be earning before they start investing in the stock market. Many people think they have to be first-cousins to Bill Gates before they start investing in the stock market, although that wouldn't hurt! On the contrary, you should start early and when you have a steady source of income. Personally, my gauge for stock investing begins when you are able to cover living and feeding expenses. If you have some extra cash after your BASIC needs have been taken care of, you should allocate the rest to investing; whether in stocks, a mortgage, real estate, money market funds or any wealth-generating vehicle.

Of course, if you have more than a couple of hundred thousand dollars liquid cash in the bank, you could be aggressive when forming your investment strategy. However, I suggest a cautious and conservative approach if you are not earning a whole lot of money; less than $40,000 annually. You must have the financial self-control to start small in your investment plan; make some gains, develop an unemotional and analytical mind when it comes to selecting your stocks and then with time, commit larger sums to stock investing.

Stock investing is an exciting and often rewarding experience for the educated and informed investor. It is my hope that you make as much money as possible through investing in the Nigerian stock market, now that you understand how it works, the other participants in the market and are in the early stages of forming an investment style that fits you.

Chapter 4
Finding the money to invest

Hey, the day has finally come! You are jumping with joy in the knowledge that you can make some money in Nigeria on Broad Street. The stocks are out there to buy, the brokers are ready to execute your trades and you have an epiphany of yourself relaxing with friends in the Bahamas sipping coconut wine under palm trees while watching the blue sky and narrating how reading this book changed your financial perspective and life. Hold up…..not so fast! Where, how and when are you going to get the money to invest? If you have some money saved in the bank strictly set aside for investing, great job. However, if you belong to the 22% bracket of the American population that have no money once they are done paying for essential items, you must be sitting in a chair wondering how to raise money not only for investing in Nigerian stocks, but paying rent to the annoying landlord, credit companies and taking care of a family, if you have one.

If you are waiting to win the lottery to finance your stock trades, good luck to you as I don't see that happening. Why? Two reasons: your odds of winning the US power ball lottery are 1 in 146,107,962 which means you have a better chance of being struck by lighting or killed in a car accident. Secondly, I think the lottery is an insulting game created by a system that gives people the illusion that they can make stupendous amounts of money by taking the little they have and making them poorer. Now that you are scratching your head and figuring the challenge of raising the cash to fund your stock investing plan; do not allow fear and anxiety bother you.

This chapter would focus strictly on assessing your financial situation, working out a feasible plan for financial freedom and determining your financial goals. There are tons of books out there that focus on personal finance and I realize that many would just want to get on with the investing game, but I feel this chapter is very relevant to your investment psyche. Investment assets can be looked at as one big cake; stocks being a slice of that cake to help you grow wealthy. If you are having problems with your entire financial cake, trust me, stock investing will not sweeten your financial bitterness. In the following pages, we will undertake a "financial checkup"; diagnose your current health status and suggest ways of improvement.

GROUND ZERO: EVALUATING YOUR CURRENT POSITION

The first step for you as an investor is to assess where you are financially. To understand how vital this step is, let us use the companies you intend investing in as an analogy. You read about a company that is engaged in the oil distribution business in Nigeria and that has grown its revenues by 35% annually for the past six years. Interesting, you think! You call your broker in Nigeria and enquire if the company is listed on the NSE, to which the broker replies in the affirmative. At this juncture, it would not be such a smart idea to go ahead and give your broker some money to buy the company's stock. You have not done your research yet (more on that in the coming chapters). You go ahead and hire an investment analyst to assess the company and report back to you on if it is a worthy investment. After the analysis is completed, you have a good idea of whether you are investing or plain dumping your money.

The same way financial analysts assess companies is the way you are going to assess your personal finances today. I will focus on YOUR balance sheet and income statements and by the time we are through combing your financial barnyard, we should be on our way to discovering the cash you need to invest with. So grab pen and paper and let's do that together right here and now.

STUDYING YOUR PERSONAL BALANCE SHEET

Have you ever wondered, "What am I worth"? And before you answer the question; someone drops a copy of *Forbes* magazine in your laps with a catchy front cover screaming "The net worth of America's Richest"!!! You flip to page 73 where all their names and correspondent net worth values are listed and realize that the 'poorest' of the group is worth $950 million! It's easy to give up asking the question after a painful reminder like that but it's important you ask the question so you can move ahead in your financial journey and hopefully join the *Forbes* list- hey, that would be awesome! A famous preacher in Nigeria, David Oyedepo, put it best: "If you don't know where you are going, how will you know if you have started the journey"?

The answer to the question is found when you draw up a balance sheet. In simple terms, the balance sheet is a snapshot of your value at any given time, matching your assets and liabilities against each other. Assets are simply items or instruments that you OWN such as real estate, stocks, bank accounts, clothes, motor vehicles and related items. Liabilities on the other hand, are items that you OWE such as mortgages, credit card debt, bank loans, taxes and unpaid bills. If your assets exceed your liabilities, it means you have a positive net worth. If liabilities outweigh assets, not so good news; you owe more than you own and actually have a negative net-worth. The name of the game is to always have a positive and growing positive net worth. An illustration of the Danladi family's balance sheet is illustrated below.

DANLADI FAMILY BALANCE SHEET

ASSETS	LIABILITIES
Two Cars - $145,000	Mortgage- $250,000
Mutual funds- $135,000	Consumer Loans- $70,000
Checking Account- $14,000	Student Loans- $56,000
Savings Account- $3,000 (5.2% rate)	Credit Cards- $20,000
TOTAL ASSETS = $297,000	**TOTAL LIABILITIES= $396,000**

NET WORTH/ (LOSS) = ASSETS- LIABILITIES= $(99,000)

From the above illustration, it is obvious that the Danladi family like a lot of folk, has a negative net worth and if they ever want to invest in the Nigerian stock market; they have to do something fast about curbing the growth in their liabilities. Composing a balance sheet like the one above is a powerful graphical tool that clearly shows you where you stand and helps you design concrete financial goals for your future. It is imperative that you know where you are you are before you can get anywhere and the balance sheet is an excellent starting point.

Some of you after drawing up your personal balance sheets would be delighted to discover that you actually have more than you originally thought. In that case, congratulations and please don't spend the extra cash you "discovered" on a trip to the Caribbean just yet! We have some investing to do, remember? If you are wondering where to find information to tally your assets and liabilities, start with your bank statements and other documents. If you feel those documents do not reflect current prices, you can seek the aid of a valuation expert to estimate what the asset is currently worth; or save yourself the expense of paying a valuation expert by using the many online price comparison tools. If you have drawn up your personal balance sheet and find yourself on the other side of the river with a negative net-worth; all it could take to get you back to a positive net-worth could be adjusting some items on the balance sheet. Let's discuss some options you could take in order to lose the weight- I mean assets and cut down your liabilities:

Distinguish a real asset from a revenue-generating asset

Looking at the Danladi family's balance sheet, you will realize that they have two cars worth $140,000 and for now let's assume one is a Mercedes Benz that is worth $68,000. Although accounting principles would list vehicles, motorbikes and other forms of transportation (you don't happen to ride a yacht to work do you?) as assets, the truth of the matter is that they are liabilities that eat deep into your pocket when you factor in expenses such as car insurance, auto-loan payments and maintenance fees. The Danladi family can work towards a positive net-worth by selling off the high-maintenance Mercedes Benz and invest it in something that actually generates more income for them. If they placed the extra cash in their mutual fund that generates 12% returns annually; they have effectively increased their assets.

Replace low-yielding investments with high yielding ones

One of the big mistakes investors make is placing their idle funds in ventures that produce little or no returns because they want to 'play it safe'. There is no such thing if you intend becoming an intelligent and successful investor. Going back to the Danladi family's balance sheet, you will realize that they have $14,000 in a checking account that generates nothing for them but only $3,000 in a savings account with a 5.2% interest rate. You might say a 5.2% rate of return will not cover the deficit the Danladi family has, but then, you will be missing the point. If you want to become an astute investor, you must be smart enough to fight for every single dollar and gain that is available to you. It is not being stingy, it means that you are financially-savvy. A little here and a little there could make you a millionaire before you realize it by investing in the best assets out there.

By shifting $10,000 from their checking account to their savings account, they would have an extra $676 dollars in their pocket in a year's time. That's money you could set aside to buy gasoline for the rest of the year (assuming you don't ride one of those humungous gas-guzzling SUVs out there!) or even better, set aside in your investment account to buy more Nigerian stocks.

Get out of debt …..And fast!

"How do I get out of debt, so I can have a positive net worth?" was the question I asked myself in graduate school with a truckload of debt hanging over my head and no tangible job in sight when something funny happened to me. My investments in the Nigerian stock market had hit an all-time high and my research (with the help of local analysts) had showed me it was time to cash out from some bank stocks. I cashed out and had a cool $4500 in my hands to play around with but then a friend of mine gave me insight into a little-known security services firm listed on the NYSE that had been ratcheting huge gains and I saw a huge opportunity to make some more money since it was a penny-stock with great valuations.

My thinking was that I could make a whole lot of money from which I could pay off my college debt. I told a financial smarter friend of mine about my dilemma and he asked a simple question: "Wale, do you have any debt?" I embarrassingly admitted that I did and he shook his head in disbelief and told me to forget about the stock and pay off my debt. I grudgingly did and I am better off for doing so. Debt could be a big clog in the wheels of your financial fortune and trust me, there are many good books that teach you how to manage and eliminate debt. For now, here is my advice.

If you have bad debt which comprises of things you do not need and cannot afford (good debt includes expenses on your mortgage and college education), please avoid the stock market until you are done paying off those credit cards and high-interest bank loans. I want to be sure that you have a sense of financial discipline before you go near the stock market. Many financial advisors would disagree with me on this subject, promising you that stock market gains could aid your debt-elimination plan. True it can happen but it is not guaranteed. How you take care of debt is totally up to you. Work two jobs, create and sell a product; do whatever you have to (as long as it is legal); all I ask is that you make a firm commitment to come out of debt before investing in the Nigerian stock market. It is a worthy exercise and will give you a sense of freedom that really satisfies.

STUDYING YOUR PERSONAL INCOME STATEMENT

An income statement is a financial document that summarizes all your revenue and expenses in a given year. You can draw up this sheet right now. Come on, let's do it together. On the sheet of paper you have pulled out, draw a two-columned table and list all sources of personal income on the left hand side of the table and expenses on the right. Your revenue income would include your salary, wages, dividends from your stock investments, rent money if you have a house that you rent out to others, business income assuming you have a full or part-time job you operate and of course, the occasional dollar you pick up on the streets (hey, I'm kidding; I know you are not that kind of person). Your expenses are items that you spend money on. On the right hand side of the sheet, list your expenses that would normally include credit card and loan payments, dinner and holiday trip payments, food, utilities, daycare charges, medical expenses and any other good or service that you spend money on.

Is it not funny how long our expenses list is compared to the income list? Do not worry about that. This book along with your desire to succeed financially would make those lines switch places! Having the income statement right in front of you showing you how much you are making and where that money is going is as important as your personal balance sheet. It is hard work since you have to get out a lot of receipts and bills to identify which item belongs where in the income statement. In the future, to simplify this process have a small cashbook where you can record your daily expenses and don't have to sound foolish again saying "I don't know where my money went"! Make a pledge to yourself to keep a tight eye on where your money goes.

If your income exceeds your expenses, I applaud you as you must be "in the black" (have a positive net income). If your expenses are more than what you earn, you are obviously in the red (negative net-income) since you are spending money you do not have to manage the difference. Obviously, in such a situation you will not have the needed funds to invest in stocks. All it would take is an adjustment and reduction of your expenses; while boosting your income to generate more cash for your pocket. It is not that difficult once you put your mind to it and determine to follow certain financial freedom steps. There are many great personal finance books at your local library that would show you how to manage your money; however allow me suggest three areas you can focus on and turn your income statement to a consistently positive balance month in, month out. Check out these income boosters.

Develop multiple streams of passive income

Many people are comfortable doing one job or even two to pay their bills and hopefully; have extra to enjoy a little bit of living. However, if your financial goal is to achieve true financial freedom; there has to be a paradigm shift in your work mentality from working hard to working smart. A good way of making money the smart way is to generate passive income. Passive income is income you generate by not being actively involved in the business. Some examples of passive income include dividends you receive from your stock investments, income from rental property and royalties from an invention or creative work of yours.

If you ever want to be wealthy (which is a noble objective, there is nothing special about being broke- trust me I've being there and it's no fun!), you have to start creating income that does not require your constant presence. Let me share a first-hand experience in the creation of passive income. My roommate in college was a reputed computer whiz-kid and was always complaining about money. After some soul-searching, he put his skills to work by designing a website where he sold data management and web hosting services; allowing people all over the world purchase his product and deposit money in his bank account while he slept. Some of you after reading this book may discover streams of income from your hobbies, just the way I did. I have always loved writing and helping people achieve their goals. By writing this book, I have created a product that can be bought through various outlets and generates royalty for me. I do not have to go around selling my book and this frees up time for me to focus on other ventures. Look around you and start exploring the passive income opportunities around you.

Pack your lunch and eat dinner at home

For the majority of us, food consumption eats up our paycheck like no other expense and unfortunately is hurting our plans to save more money. If you are a huge Starbucks fan, here's a bit of information that could help you: If you bought a latte everyday for $3.20 per cup for the next 30 years, you would have spent $35,040. If that money had being invested in a mutual fund or placed in a fixed deposit with an annual rate of 15%, that money over the same 30 year period would turn out $2.3 million! Can you imagine what you could do with $2.3 million when you retire?

With food accounting for 15% to 50% of some household incomes (obviously you would spend a higher proportion of your income on food if you earn $35,000 annually, in comparison to a family that has a total household income over $150,000), many people are struggling to save and understandably so. The plan to earn more money from food cost-savings is a challenge but you know what? You can do it! All it takes is some adjustment in your lifestyle, eating habits and perspective of where your money goes. I have some tips that helped me and others in this regard, let me share them with you.

Make a budget for food expenses well in advance of going to the grocery store. By knowing what you need in advance of walking through the grocery aisle, you will effectively cut down on impulse purchases (usually unnecessary) and convenience foods (always expensive). A budget would help you track where your money goes in the food department and help you buy in large quantities that are always less expensive than smaller purchases of the same foods that you buy almost weekly.

Use coupons even if you are afraid that your coworker 'accidentally' sneaks behind you at the check-out counter and snickers when she sees the bundle of clippings dangling from your hands like spaghetti strings! Coupons save millions of people (smart enough to spend a few minutes everyday to clip them off) precious dollars that could be invested in something that actually generates wealth for them.

Shop at the cheapest grocery store out there. Don't you think it makes sense to save a dollar when you can? Surveys indicate that in many cities, the price differential between stores in the same area could be as high as 30%! The other thing about the cheapskate grocery store is that they usually offer generic products that are usually the same as those in snazzier looking stores, so there's point spending extra on the same.

Including nutritious foods in your diets. Of course, good genes and exercise are a plus for some of us that can eat anything. However, adding healthier foods such as fruits and vegetables to your diet can seriously boost your health and save a bundle on healthcare costs. It is estimated that close to $155 billion in medical expenses in the United States are direct results of a poor diet. Apart from attaining that sexy body that you always see on late-night infomercials from eating right, you would add some serious cash in your wallet in healthcare cost-savings when you start eating right!

Watch car costs

At the time this book went to press, global oil prices had climbed by over 200% in a six year period and to say that the pinch on our collective purses has been excruciating, would be an understatement. Inflation is also on the rise so you are actually getting less gas at a higher price; unfortunately, oil prices seem to be on an uncontrollable surge. In a society where having a car is a necessity; we must be smart about the amount of money that goes towards these mechanical contraptions that guzzle gas like a starved man in the Sahara desert seeing a half-glass of water. There are a couple of ways to minimize the rising cost of gas that removes money from your pocket. Let's take a look at some of them.

Buy a used car. You might go "Duh, I know that already Wale". If you do, that's great. Some of you have to change your mentality believing that driving a new car is the ultimate experience for you. Sit down and let me talk to you. A car is a mere mechanical contraption that takes you from Point A to Point B. It might make a 'statement' to some people but that is irrelevant when you still have credit card debt, a huge mortgage and college loans to pay off (God help you, if you already have kids that got admitted into Ivy-league schools last week)! If you are living in this state of impressing others, while depressing yourself; it is high time that you do a reality check on yourself and start thinking of buying a used car. The benefits of a used car are enormous. Used cars are normally cheaper than new cars (duh, again!), giving you extra savings that could go into other investments. They depreciate slower and maintain their reliability (unlike brand new cars that depreciate by 25% immediately you drive them off the dealer's lot). Used cars involve lesser costs unlike the torrent of fees you have to pay on insurance and licensing for new vehicles.

Go for an affordable fuel-efficient vehicle. In America, the Sports Utility Vehicle (SUV) is the most admired vehicle that has found its way into millions of garages. The problem is that it costs so much to fill the tank and if you have one, be honest and admit it's a gas-guzzler. Now if you are making enough money to cover gassing your SUV, great. If not, why not explore the option of a smaller vehicle with higher gas economy. It might be hard for you to let go of your beloved SUV, the one you like to pull up besides smaller vehicles and condescendingly look down upon (oops....if you are not smiling right now, you know I'm talking about you)! Trading in for a smaller and fuel-efficient vehicle would save you a bundle that could fund your Nigerian stock investing plan.

Go environmental and save big. Okay, that sounds like an ad slogan for an environmental group but it's true. Think of it. Have you thought about walking to the grocery store or riding the bus or metro to work for some time? If you live in a drive-through society such as ours were sitting down in your car to get anywhere and do everything is no longer the exception but the norm, your answer is likely to be in the negative. You know what? Except you live in some far-flung city or town that lacks a good metropolitan transportation system, you are burning precious dollars that could be generating cash for your personal investment program. The only exceptions to the prior statement should be physical difficulty or that you are a highly-priced human target for criminals. Now you know that you can save by doing the above, so why don't you? Maybe you need a little math to show you the reality of the money that goes up in the air by sticking to driving your vehicle all the time. For example, if it costs you about $150 a month in gas expenses; you will be spending a whooping $54,000 on gas in only thirty years. However, if you rode the bus or metro three times a week; you could slash that amount by half to $27,000 Using the 30 year model from our 'latte example' earlier on, if you invested $27,000 in a mutual fund that generated 15% annual returns over 30 years; it turns into $1.8 million. Also the health benefits of walking are great (plus you will have some strong and nice-looking legs along the way)! But can you see how much money you can make by cutting down on gas purchases. If you are 25 years old now, you do not even need a financial planner to help you figure out that this would help you live a more satisfied life when you start contemplating retirement. You might also get a kick out of creating wealth for yourself while contributing to a better environment.

Building a financial future for yourself would take a lot of planning and discipline on your part. You may falter at times but if you stick these simple suggestions, you will generate more cash to sustain your personal and investment needs. I mean now that you've got the money, the next thing to do is to invest it right? Well, after a little research on the companies listed on the NSE don't you think? Correct. Flip the page and I will introduce you to the importance of financial research on your investment decisions.

Chapter 5
Research, research and some more research!

You pick up the morning paper and the business section has a screaming headline declaring "KBZ Oil up 350% and still climbing!" You shake your head in disbelief and turn on the TV only to hear a financial analyst speaking about KBZ and its plans to invest $400 million on exploration on two oil fields in the Niger Delta that have proven reserves of a billion barrels. As you drive to work, you start thinking about KBZ Oil and the possibility of investing in a company that seems to have a profitable future. After all, you still have your $25,000 bonus from last year doing nothing in a savings account that returns 2.6% annually and a little of that money in KBZ stock could make you a millionaire you think. At work, all your coworkers are calling their brokers at lunchtime to load up on KBZ stock like crazy. You suddenly get a strong feeling that you are about to miss out on another amazing investment opportunity (remember you refused to take Bill Gates' call when he needed investors in 1981) and call your Lagos-based broker to buy $20,000 worth of KBZ.

Now the story above is fiction and please do not invest in KBZ Oil except such a company comes into existence someday! You might feel that your stock buying decision can never follow the path described above but surprisingly that is exactly what millions of investors do on a daily basis- buy stocks strictly on hearsay and Wall Street or should I say Broad Street financed hype. Doing so is a classic example of a misinformed investment strategy that relies more on 'market sentiments' rather than an unbiased appraisal of the financial condition of the company you wish to invest in. The way to go about this appraisal is by conducting a fundamental analysis of your prospective stock.

Fundamental analysis is an interesting sounding process that simply uses financial and economic data to analyze a company, so as to assess and forecast the value of the company's stock. It examines the underlying factors that influence that particular company. Some of those factors include the political climate, changes in the specific industry, competitive pressure from other companies, exchange rate changes; even the weather. Gathering mounds of financial documents from a thousand sources is no easy task. If you think that's tough, try the fun stuff financial analysts do- actually reading those boring documents and some more documents that the office intern proudly found on the internet! Making the effort to dig deep into a business' financial statements is time-consuming, brain tasking but worth it, especially as it helps you discover companies that have real and sustainable value. However, to be practical since you probably have a job and other personal commitments that demand a great deal of your time; it makes sense for you to leverage your access to available investment research and financial documents that are already out there. Let us look at some key research documents you must have in your investment library and see how some concepts will help you select winning stocks and avoid the trap of buying hyped stocks like KBZ Oil!

SOURCING INVESTMENT RESEARCH

The beauty of available investment research is that the nitty-gritty task of number-crunching and analysis has already been performed by many analysts and the financial documents that showcase the facts behind the company can be found in company annual reports. Research reports, also known as investment reports are produced by brokerages, business research firms and investment banks to assess the target company's financial condition and forecast the possible future of the company under various scenarios. These reports are prepared by trained professionals called financial analysts (or investment analysts) who normally have business degrees and experience in the securities industry.

In the US, many top research firms have financial analysts that possess a Certified Financial Analyst (CFA) designation which is a respected industry-standard for analyzing the financial condition of companies. In Nigeria, there are a growing number of CFA holders that produce research for investors particularly those that reside abroad. However, there is no Nigerian body that certifies financial analysts to produce research reports. Most research in the country is produced by seasoned finance professionals using the same methodologies found globally, many of whom are licensed to practice auditing and stock broking by the Institute of Chartered Accountants of Nigeria (ICAN) and the Chartered Institute of Stockbrokers (CIS) respectively. Annual reports can be sourced directly from the companies you are interested. All you need to do is call the corporate affairs department of the specific company that interests you or call your broker to retrieve a copy. Another excellent source for financial documents you should try is the Nigerian SEC office.

You might be a student, professional or contemplating retirement soon, and from your experience in life; understand the value of time in today's fast-paced world. If you have enough free time to engage in meticulous evaluation of companies that pique your interest, go for it. For those of you with professional and personal commitments, you might not have that luxury and may require a miracle to squeeze in two or thee hours a week to go over all the documents you can find on a company yourself. Financial analysis is not rocket-science but definitely time consuming for a busy individual like yourself; it makes sense then to place some confidence in the analysis of seasoned finance analysts that can summarize the relevant information on a listed company and provide a decent recommendation why the investment should be considered or avoided. The research reports produced by analyst could appear as rocket science but are rather easy to understand once you read a couple of them. Many of the reports produced in Nigeria by top brokerages and independent research companies are designed in the same format as the popular *Value Line Investment Surveys* produced in the United States.

HOW TO READ A RESEARCH REPORT

Financial analysts across the globe research thousands, even millions of companies each year and their reports help investors like you and I make an informed judgment on listed companies. Fund and money managers also use this vital service to make investment decisions involving billions of dollars in managed assets. The research arm of Nigerian investment banks and brokerage firms provide independent research reports on companies listed on the Nigerian stock market, some of which are free when you sign up for a brokerage account or other service they provide; others can be purchased at a reasonable fee. When you start investing in Nigerian stocks, ask your broker if the firm they work for offers research reports and daily updates. If not, I highly recommend you use a broker that does.

The greatest benefit of research reports is that they provide a snapshot of the most critical information that helps you make quick decisions, the majority of them being summarized in a page or two. To understand the beneficial leverage an investment report provides in the selection of quality stocks, you must approach studying the research reports from a value investor's perspective. A value investor is the type of investor that looks at the value of the company and judges if the stock price is fair enough to place a buy order. Research reports are basically compiled from historical data so you must not be given to the nuances of "projections" that guide some people's investment plans. It is a common saying that "wise men look at the past to predict the future". That statement holds true for stock investments as a steady financial track record of your target stock should be a guiding light for possible performance in the future. Many research reports have brief snapshots of a company's financial figures for the preceding five years. The relevance of this information to your investment decision cannot be underestimated as the numbers may reveal if the company is growing, stagnant or decreasing in value over time.

Most of the information in research reports is extracted from the company's annual report, analysis done on the financial figures and key statistics mined out that paint a brief but incisive picture of the financial health of the company. Now, all this stuff might sound mind-boggling; particularly if you are like many of us that do not like numbers. Do not worry; I will introduce you to the key sections of a research report that are really important. Before you think that the information is too stale to be of any use to you, you have to realize that most reports are updated often by good research providers; so you would not be exactly dealing with research from the Stone Age! Reading a research report is like reading an inspirational history book because it's all stuff that happened in the past but useful to you when making decisions in the present that have an impact on your future. Quality reports are normally scattered with graphs and prose that could make you delirious but I want you to focus on eight parts of the report that ultimately frame your personal opinion on the stock.

1. Business Profile

The business profile of the research report serves as an introduction of the company to you by the analyst. It basically describes the company's business and its position in its industry. For example, if you read a research report on Microsoft, the business profile of the company would state something similar to this: "Established in 1975, Microsoft Corporation is involved in the development, manufacture, and support and licensing of software products for electronic computing devices in markets around the world. The company is divided into seven divisions that specifically service the needs of the market segments the company serves. Headquartered in Redmond Washington, Microsoft employs 61,000 people around the world and generated revenues of $39.8 billion in 2005". Some research reports may have longer or shorter company profiles but the key components focus on the size of the company, the stake of senior executives and directors in the company (this is important so you realize just how much vested interest the managers have in the company, which is a good indicator of their commitment to the company), and the names of principal executives of the company. Knowing the names of the company's senior management helps you monitor these individuals, particularly if their professional and personal conduct influences your investment in the company.

2. Market Capitalization

As unromantic as it sounds, the market capitalization of a company is considered one of the most important pieces of information financial analysts look at. In simple language, market capitalization refers to the value of the company you are investing in. To calculate the market cap (financial jargon for market capitalization): all you have to do is multiply the current stock price by the number of outstanding shares issued. For example, if you wanted to know the market cap of Guaranty Trust Bank of Nigeria; all you do is find out how many shares the company issued; pick up your local newspaper and locate the price at which GTB closed on the NSE for that day; multiply the two figures and voila, you have your market capitalization! So if GTB has issued 1.5 billion shares and its stock price closed at $0.13 today, its market capitalization would be 1.5 billion shares multiplied by $0.13 which gives us a sum of $195 million.

Knowing the size of a company's market cap over a period of time is useful as it indicates the growth patterns of the company. In the 1980s, the market cap of software giant Microsoft was in the $15 billion range; today, the company is valued at over $280 billion. If the market cap of your prospective target is going down, you should realize that you might be engaging in a risky investment. Reasons for the drop might be totally accidental, but chances are higher that the company is not properly managed or there is a declining market for its products or services; which causes other investors to bail out on the company. Don't be left holding the bag! Another benefit to knowing the market cap of your target company is that it helps you compare the size of the company to others in its industry. So if you have Company A with a market cap of $4 billion and Company B valued at $2.5 billion, you understand that Company A is definitely bigger and would probably have a larger market share for its products or services. One thing I want you to study when you start trading on the NSE is the growth pattern of a company's market cap overtime, preferably over a 10 year period. If a small bank's market cap has been growing by about 35% annually and is valued at $400 million and there is a bigger bank with a market cap of $4.5 billion with a 2% annual growth rate; it is obvious that the smaller bank is growing faster and you should be able to make a judgment call on whether you want to stick with a growing and profitable company or a slow-moving beast.

3. Asset Valuation

Stock trading as I always say is one of the most exciting professions any one can engage in, whether full-time or part-time; particularly if you are winning and making some serious cash to flaunt around the neighborhood in your brand new Ferrari vehicle! Making informed and intelligent trades are another ballgame especially when you have a couple of companies in a particular industry that you are interested in but having a hard time selecting the one which could earn you decent returns (like a beautiful woman would have a hard time choosing a husband if she was allowed to select one out of the ten most handsome men in the world. Tough don't you think?) Knowing the book value of a company's assets- things like its buildings, vehicles, and equipment and manufacturing plants; would help you decipher the intrinsic value of a company.

The book value refers to the amount the company would get if it sold all its assets. To gain a better understanding of the book value, imagine your target company has various assets and was on its way out of business and decided to sell all its assets during liquidation for the exact amount it initially paid for it. Supposing total receipts from the sale of all assets amounts to $200 million; that is the book value. Book value is usually calculated net of depreciation. However, relying on this number is not advisable due to apparent changes in the value of certain assets. For example, real estate is known to increase in value overtime in stable housing markets; while vehicles and manufacturing plants depreciate. Using the information from annual reports, financial analysts calculate the effects of depreciation and appreciation on company assets and can give you the true market value of the company's assets.

What use is the market value to your stock investment? Well, the market value helps you know if the company's net worth is appreciating, decreasing or stagnant. In a situation where the company goes under and the company is liquidated, it is always good news to know you will get some money back from the company in the event of liquidation or bankruptcy, and the assets finally sold. If the company's market value tends to have decreased over a period of time; it makes sense for you to avoid such a stock and focus on other growing companies.

4. Stock Performance

Many research reports usually have a graph that shows the movement in price of a company's stock over a certain period of time. The graph could cover a period of time as far back as ten years or days. It is possible to get stock updates every 15 minutes on companies traded on the major markets such as the NYSE or the London Stock Exchange. The peak and lowest points on the graph indicate the highest and lowest price of the stock over the given period. When reading the report, make sure you follow the timeline that surrounds price movement to deduct if the stock is vulnerable to market and industry news. Take the example of news affecting Cadbury Nigeria, the biggest confectionary company in the country whose flagship chocolate product *Bournvita* takes a hit from an increase in government taxes on cocoa production; while struggling to maintain its current production capacity and fend off competition from an upcoming chocolate brand of another competitor. What do you think would happen to Cadbury Nigeria's stock? Well, there are no guarantees that the following would happen but likely effects of such a scenario may lead to higher costs for Cadbury Nigeria which depresses company profits, lowers dividends to shareholders, diversion of money budgeted to boost capacity to pay off taxes and other payments, erosion of market share and eventual shareholder fatigue over the stock.

Being able to gauge how that kind of news over a specific time frame and watch its influence over the stock price is an art that you must develop quickly. Looking at price performance over periods of time could help you gauge potential movements in price that could assist you make a fairly good guess of what direction the stock is headed in. In Nigeria, most reports would show stock price movements as a graph usually over a sliding six-month period. Depending on your financial advisor in Nigeria, you can actually request that they provide a customized report for you at an additional fee. If you are a cheapskate like many of us, you could simply access free price data graphs from London-based SBA Research Group that tracks the stock movement of listed companies in Africa and the Middle East.

5. Trading Volume

If you have had the opportunity of watching stock analysts on TV, you may have heard one of them say: "The company's trading volume is the issue" What they are actually referring to is the average amount of a company's shares traded over a period of time; usually calculated daily, monthly, quarterly or annually. For clarification, let us use the example of ABC Shipping that has a total amount of 100 million shares outstanding and on a given day, 15 million of those shares are traded. That means the daily trading volume is 15% of outstanding common shares and some research reports would indicate the average trading volume of a stock over different time frames.

Using this information, you will be able to decide which companies have healthy trading scenarios. This is important because if a company has low trading volumes constantly, it's a dog- please ditch it fast! Stocks with low trading volumes will kill your investment portfolio because they are easily affected by the emergence of bad news and overtime have experienced huge price crashes. The greatest challenge an investor faces with stocks trading at low volumes are their characteristic point fluctuation. These fluctuations occur because there is a mismatch in the economics of trading that particular stock, since there is no guarantee that there would be a buyer or seller for the stock; since the wider stock market is not interested in the stock. This is bad news for an investor who has already purchased the stock because if he cannot find a buyer, he would be left holding on to a stock that nobody wants! Many investors are concerned with stock prices to the point that they totally ignore volume as an important determinant while picking stocks. In actual fact, understanding market volume would put you in a different league of Nigerian stock investors; since average trading volume is an excellent gauge of investor interest and the direction of the market.

Healthy companies on the NSE should have large trading volumes and if followed by large percentage increases in the stock price, may be signaling that the company stock has gained market strength and respect amongst investors. Now some analysts will scream at my generalization but this book is more of an introductory investment guide rather than a technical analysis manual (a professional financial advisor could help you out there), so let me redeem myself by saying that good picks are out there even when they have low volumes. Those kinds of companies may be in emerging markets with new business models and it may take time for the larger market to recognize their value. However, I advise that you act in consultation with your financial advisor to determine if such a company's stock is worth buying.

6. Insider Activity

Every time the word "insider" appears on the TV screen or you hear the newscaster mention it, it sounds so mysterious and unconsciously, the first thing that pops into our minds is the possibility of insider trading occurring in a company. Insider trading refers to the buying and selling of a company's stock by the "powers that be", namely executive and non-executive directors, officers and holders of more than ten percent of the company's total stock. Insider trading is generally viewed by the investing public in most countries as an illegal activity where these privileged company officials and majority stockholders use their massive vaults of cash to trade huge blocks of stocks, based on valuable information that the general public does not have access to till much later when that information may be irrelevant to helping the investor make an informed and profitable trade. Actually, insider trading is perfectly legal if conducted under the strict requirements of the Securities and Exchange Commission.

A typical research report would tell you the stock holdings of the big players so you can effectively gauge the impact their trades could have on the performance of the stock. Interesting members of the clique of insiders in Nigeria today are the emerging mutual funds managed by the largest investment banks and securities firms in the country. Some of these funds have deep pockets that allow them buy significant stakes in Nigerian companies and the manner in which they trade in selected stocks could make or break the stock. Look out for the percentage of shareholdings held by the insider group, whether they are company executives or institutional shareholders such as mutual funds and asset management firms. The general rule (and please don't quote me on this one) is that if insider holdings increase over a period of time; the insiders have information that could translate into increased profitability and higher stock prices. If the opposite happens, call your broker and discuss exit options; that stock might be going nowhere fast!

Although it has happened in the past that insider groups have conducted spurious buying so as to pull investors like us into an even more illogical buying frenzy, the probability of behind the scenes deal making are most likely in the offing that you should be aware of. Unfortunately for investors, insider trading data in Nigeria is not as accessible as in the United States where you can visit the website of the SEC for such information. Until you probably have to employ the services of a brokerage that has access to such insider trading information and can communicate it to you in good time, you will have to wing this one and trade based on the fundamentals of the business and news reports of significant stock sales.

Another thing to watch out for is the weak regulation of Nigeria's SEC when it comes to insider trading. Unlike the United States that responded to the massive scale of conflicted research and unbridled insider trading on Wall Street with the Sarbanes Oxley Act of 2002, Nigeria's SEC as at the publication of this book does not have a strong policy on the issue. This is a serious issue as insider trading does occur on the NSE and some industry experts would affirm that it is more rampant than most people think. At this point, do not allow the information lead you on a crusade for regulatory reform in the Nigerian stock market. Remember that you are reading this book to take advantage of whatever the situation in Nigeria is, so you can make money in this market. Follow the insider trade trail and relish the look on your friends' faces when they ask you how you did it!

7. Industry Overview

Not all research reports have a section dedicated to reviewing what is going on in the industry and how the company you are investing in performs in comparison to the competition. A decent report should do that and state the position of your company in the market; using an important concept called Market Share. Just as the name implies, market share refers to the segment of the product or service market that is controlled by your company. Duh! Seriously, it is. The company's market share is usually calculated from its revenue from a given year as a part of the total industry's revenues.

For example, the brewery industry in Nigeria has many participants but two of them stand out; Guinness Nigeria and the Nigerian Breweries Company. If you are interested in investing in those stocks, you might want to know where those companies stand individually and if their market share gives them a strong footing in the overall beverage industry and if such market share can be sustained. Supposing Guinness Nigeria has a market share of 32% and Nigerian Breweries has a 25% market share in 2005, it would be easy to think that Guinness Nigeria would be a winner- and that assumption would be right, because market dominance usually translates into sustainable and profitable investments. However, as I said earlier you must study the past to predict the future to uncover value. Reviewing more research reports and documents, you might discover that the market share of Nigerian Breweries increased from 15% to 25% within a five year period and that the company is investing in more production plants across the country and its marketing campaign amongst the drinking public (that sounds wrong doesn't it?), you would realize that the real and potential market share growth is found in Nigerian Breweries. Golden rule: buy a stock because of its potential for future growth; never be impressed by its current performance.

Some analysts would focus on potential and growing competition in the industry and could suggest other companies that might be tomorrow's winners. Industry overviews also provide news on what goes on in the market, economy and regulatory environment that could influence the performance of your prospective stock. It could be a new government policy that could significantly reduce the tax burden or production costs of the company, shift in the demographics of the company's target market or some other event. The importance of the industry news is important particularly in Nigeria where news is not as accessible and delivered real-time as in more sophisticated markets. The adage goes: "If you are reading about it, it is no longer news"; that statement is sage-like advice in the Nigerian financial industry. Your financial advisor in Nigeria, who is most likely to be your broker, would be a valuable source of critical news for you. If standard reports from your broker do not contain detailed industry overviews, you could commission them to prepare customized reports for a fee.

8. Analyst Assessment & Opinion

As earlier discussed, financial analysts are responsible for the overall evaluation of the financial condition of companies; which serve as the basis for their recommendation on the stock. Their assessment normally provides answers that could guide your investing decision. A lot of work is put into the equity analysis process than most investors realize as financial analysts cover hundreds, if not thousands of financial documents, just to come up with a brief and easy-to-understand research report. Many diligent analysts normally conduct what is called a company visit where they actually visit the company's headquarters, tour their facilities, inspect products, study service delivery processes and meet with key management. Such action provides them with first-hand information on the company and makes their research more reliable than that of an analyst sitting in a cubicle somewhere in another country that does not even know what country the company is located! Now call me biased but I am of the strong opinion that you should enlist a local financial analyst in Nigeria to provide you with research. If the analyst is based in the US or Europe, he better have a track record of researching Nigerian companies before recommending anything to you. There are so many issues analysts outside Nigeria do not understand and usually serve as research but it is often riddled with inaccuracies and false assumptions. Trust me, you do not want to take the chance of trading in a foreign country on poor research. There are a number of investment banks and firms that have emerging market analysts who have contact with Nigerian experts in the country. They are the ones you should approach if you prefer an independent perspective here in the United States.

    The analyst would paint a picture of the company's future for you based on the information available to them and issue a rating to sum up an opinion of that particular stock. Analyst ratings are categorized as a BUY, HOLD or SELL. The problem with ratings is that various brokerages may have different recommendations for you. So analyst X recommendation on Texaco Nigeria stock could be a BUY, while analyst Z suggests you SELL. What is an investor supposed to do in times like these? Simply gather all the information you can, conduct your own analysis and see if you find common ground with the proven analysts with superior stock-picking track records. Remember that research reports are not the Holy Grail of stock investing, just an important piece. Analyst ratings are opinions and not guaranteed statements. Hey, if you take the time to look at the bottom of research reports, you would catch the caveat that goes a little like this. "This report does not constitute an offer to trade in the stock of the company reviewed, ratings should not be considered as advice and investment decisions should not be made solely on analyst ratings". That is not to say that analysts do not guarantee their work, it simply means you have to gather data elsewhere and make the critical stock picking decision yourself.

FUNDAMENTAL ANALYIS: STICKING TO WHAT MAKES SENSE

Let me share another itsy bitsy secret of ours in the financial world: a lot of money is made off people who are easily impressed by graphs. Huh? Think about if for a minute. Have you ever gone to talk with your financial advisor or listened to some analyst and watched them mesmerize you with all these charts, with very grotesque looking numbers and phrases like "candlesticks" and at the end of their confusing speech, nodded your head in agreement and dashed out before they realize that life is already tough enough without throwing in some more confusing stuff! Most of those graphs come from an intensive process called Technical Analysis, performed by super-smart analysts who study tons of statistics that range from volume sheets, historical prices, price movements and other stuff to predict where the market is going. Great job but it could be very irrelevant for an investor like you. I suggest you and I just KISS. Not the kissy mushy *muaw* type, I mean **K**eep **I**t **S**hort and **S**imple!

The alternative is to conduct Fundamental Analysis which studies your prospective stock based on plain economic, financial and other qualitative and quantitative information. Fundamental analysts use all these factors, study what is happening inside and outside the country; to determine what the impact would be on your stock. It is a form of analysis that you can do if you have basic math skills and can relate what happens in the news to how it affects your investments. Couple your own opinion of what might happen with the ratios and key statistics you source from a research report and you would be fine. It is that simple. In my final semester at Wichita State, my instructor told me to prepare a paper on fundamental analysis and the name that kept popping up constantly when I conducted my research was that of Warren Buffett.

The most famous billionaire investor of our time, Warren Buffett, is an avid believer of fundamental analysis. His philosophy to stock investing is pretty simple: Select companies that offer a service the market needs, led by experienced and committed managers, have a track record of positive cash flows and consistent earnings, little or no debt and have a guaranteed business model for the next ten years. There are too many things going on in your life for you to be bothered by following truckloads of charts and racking your brain on the next exotic term some analyst would label a stock. Focus on the bigger picture which is the company itself rather than the stock, study the surrounding business and competitive environment, save time, invest and make money. Sounds like a plan, don't you think?

A NOTE ON ANNUAL REPORTS

It is amazing how finance professionals such as my humble self have succeeded in scaring the rest of the world when it comes to financial analysis and investing in general. Sure enough, there are some aspects of the trade that demand rigorous academic training and industry experience; but for the most part, a basic understanding of financial terms and analysis would put you ahead of the class. If you wonder where you will get the information to conduct your own financial analysis, look no further than that glossy and bulky literature your company sometimes sends in the mail called an Annual Report. The annual reports of publicly traded companies in Nigeria are prepared using accounting practices as determined by the Nigerian Accounting Standards Board (NASB), an independent agency responsible for the development and issuance of Statements of Accounting Standards for companies, financial analysts, persons that engage in the preparation of financial statements, government entities and the investing public.

Unlike the GAAP (Generally Accepted Accounting Principles) adopted in the United States and elsewhere, Nigerian accounting standards differ due to the peculiarity of its economy and regulatory environment. This information is important if and when you decide to employ the services of a financial analyst or advisor to help you make an investment decision. Nigerian law makes all other accounting standards subordinate to its own, so in simple words; an analyst in the US conducting analysis on a Nigerian company using GAAP standards could make some wrong assumptions because he is using a totally different standard for his analysis! In my opinion, get a Nigerian accountant or one based in your country that understands Nigerian accounting practices and preferably has certification in Nigerian accounting methods.

In the interim, if you would like to conduct some analysis, which is always a exciting and knowledge enriching experience if you are not a trained finance person but want the confidence of knowing you could do the job yourself; get the annual report of the company you are interested in. Many Nigerian companies have their annual reports posted on their websites and you can retrieve a hard copy by contacting the company's registrar or requesting one from your broker. Now that you have this bulky document with pictures of smiling company executives, crazy looking graphs and more numbers than you ever imagined; what do you do? Personally, I think annual reports are some of the most boring documents ever known to mankind but if your aim is to make some serious money from companies that could shape your financial future; it should be an interesting read! Do not get bogged down with irrelevant information, just focus on the key sections and you will be in good shape. If there are aspects of an annual report that you do not understand, ask your accountant or financial advisor to help you out.

The first section of most annual reports shows smiling senior company officials like the company chairman and CEO stating the performance of the company in the past financial year, the report of auditors who review the company's financial documents and ascertain if the information therein is accurate and a couple of highlights with colorful graphics to take your attention away from the main subject of your investigation: the financial details of the company's operations in the past period. The annual reports of Nigerian companies just like any other around the world will provide three important documents that show the true financial state of the company, no matter what management has to say. These documents are the company balance sheet, income and cash flow statements. If you seek a better understanding of financial statements analysis, consult your local library for literature on the subject. If you seek a simple-to-understand book on the matter, try Anthony Rice's *Accounts Demystified: How to Understand Financial Accounting and Analysis* or *Selecting Winning Stocks using Financial Statements* written by Richard Loth. However, we will briefly touch on what these documents are all about and the benefits of studying them when they come in the mail.

Balance Sheet

The balance sheet is a snapshot of the company summarizing its assets, liabilities and shareholders' equity at a particular period. Taking a cue from what we covered in Chapter 4 on evaluating your personal financial status, companies do exactly the same thing; however on a much larger scale. Company balance sheets allow you the investor understand what the company owns and what it has borrowed from creditors to run its operations; as well as the amount of money contributed by investors in the form of stocks.

Assets are what the company uses for its operations and that includes factory plants, machinery, cash assets, accounts receivable, marketable securities, inventory, notes receivable, land and office buildings. **Liabilities** on the other hand represent the portion of those assets owned by the firm that are actually owed to creditors. These liabilities could include items like accounts payable, notes payable, dividend payable, income taxes and wages payable. The interesting thing about liabilities is that in the event that a company runs into financial difficulty and is forced to shut down and sell its assets, creditors of the business (like banks and corporate bond holders) are adjudged as primary claimants; which simply means they get paid during the liquidation period before. The third arm of the balance sheet is called **shareholders' equity** which refers to the amount of money shareholders have staked in the company. Equity owners are categorized as residual claimants because they receive what is left of the company after the company's creditors have been paid.

Therefore, the balance sheet formula would look something like this:

Assets = Liabilities + Shareholders' Equity

The rule in accounting is that both sides of the equation should balance each other out. I guess it is simple logic to calculate that a company can not own more than what it has borrowed from creditors as loans and equity invested by shareholders. The balance sheet is vital to your analysis as it shows you the resources available to the company at any point in time and if the company is actually positioned to implement the strategy that management is always talking about. Financial analysts usually apply ratios using industry parameters and comparison with competing firms to help investors decide if the company can actually achieve growth projections touted by management and has no liquidity problems (a negative situation where a company does not enough have money to cover short-term debts to its creditors). Called ratio analysis, these numbers are usually calculated over a period of time as an indicator of company performance. Although financial ratios are not the all-in-all of fundamental analysis, they provide strong warning signals that you should not ignore. Consult your accountant or financial advisor to make sure that these financial ratios are well within the context of industry standards; and of course, if what I am saying right now makes absolutely no sense to you!

Income Statement

The income statement which is also known as the profit and loss statement is an important financial document that shows a company's revenues and expenses over a period of time. Although it is a popular feature of the annual report, most Nigerian companies file quarterly income statements. Company revenues are the bread and butter of every company and the income statement shows where and how the company makes its money, and how it eventually spends that money. To get revenue figures, multiply the price of the company's goods and services by the quantity of goods and services sold. Expenses are outflows from the company to pay for the goods and services that they in turn purchase and pay others, including the government in the form of taxes. Common expenses companies have to pay for include utilities, salaries, rental fees and many other types of charges. By deducting expenses from revenue, the company obtains its net income. The formula is illustrated below:

Net Income = Revenue − Expenses

On the flipside if expenses exceed revenue, the company will naturally experience a loss as illustrated by the following equation:

Net Loss = Expenses − Revenue

The income statement helps you track the real financial management of the company and answers questions such as: Has the company created new products or services to generate more revenue? Why are expenses increasing rapidly? Have profits been growing, stable or decreasing and how can we improve on current numbers? Knowing the answers would be very useful to you in deciding what companies are deserving of your hard-earned money. An important fall-out of analyzing the income statement is that you have to remember to focus on uncovering the future value of the company. If the company announces huge profits, that is a good sign; however, the value of buying that stock really kicks in for you only if you had purchased it earlier.

Let us consider the example of an imaginary *Lakeside Bank*. If you have been tracking the stock for 15 months and notice that the company has managed to lower its overall expenses, launched two financial products that millions of Nigerians like because of the juicy saving rates, negotiated lower tax payments with the Federal Inland Revenue Service and received a $100 million injection from a partner bank abroad to boost its branch expansion plans to 20 more cities in the coming year; it does not take a rocket scientist to tell you that Lakeside Bank is positioned for growth and you could make huge bucks! If you buy Lakeside stocks way early when they are dirt cheap, you will be way ahead of the crowd when they are excited at the huge profit potential of Lakeside. By that time, the market would have factored in the profit potential of the bank and the share price would have gone up, causing others to buy high. The example might be simplistic because there are still many good stocks in any market that are undervalued even though the financial statements look good. For the most part, this happens regularly and underscores the advantage you get by studying the income statement for your own benefit.

Cash flow Statement

The last member of the "three musketeer sheets" as I like to call them, is the charming cash flow statement. A cash flow statement provides financial data on the company's cash inflows obtained from its revenue generating operations and cash outflows paid in the course of doing business and investing in assets that will generate future growth for the company. The distinct feature of the cash flow statement from other financial documents is that it reports the actual cash available to the company. Unlike the income statement which includes non-accounting items, the cash flow statement disregards such items and focuses strictly on the king himself. No, not Elvis, I am talking about CASH. Still confused? Let me break it down for you.

See those spectacular revenues declared on quarterly and annual income statements? Some of them include revenue that has not been actually collected because the goods sold were sold on credit and some customers are yet to pay up, and until that money has been collected from customers, the company actually has less cash than seen on the income statement. So although a company might be declaring net profits of $500 million; the cash flow statement may show that it only has $200 million available. Don't get riled at the creative tendencies of the accounting profession, that's just the way it is. However, you are in luck as the cash flow statement is in your corner giving you a clearer picture of the cash position of your target company. From an analytical standpoint, it clarifies the ability of the company to pay its bills on time. This is so important to you as an investor because it would be a bummer to invest in a company that does not have the actual cash to implement the growth strategy that management has in place. Unfortunately, there are too many analysts out there screaming on television about the earnings of a company that many investors get caught with their pants down buying stock in companies that are clearly unable to pay dividends when due and make the strategic steps that would boost performance. However, a negative cash flow statement may not be an indication of imminent doom if such a negative occurs because the company invested a substantial sum that year on expansion projects. Be mindful of analyzing the company as a stand-alone, the best option is to compare its cash position with competitors in its industry. If it is not, ditch it and pick a winner.

Chapter 6
Selecting a Stockbroker

If you have ever wanted to send a container load of golf clubs to a business partner living on the other side of the world, has it ever crossed your mind that you could just buy a ship, hire a crew and deliver the merchandise yourself? Now we both know that really wouldn't make economic sense if shipping the clubs cost you only $35,000 while a small transport ship could burn a $500,000 hole in your pocket; except you simply have a load of cash to burn and that would mean you are overqualified to be reading this book! For the rest of humanity, it makes sense to go through an individual or company that is qualified and capable of completing the transaction with as little hassle on your part. In the same vein, after you have concluded researching Nigerian companies and decided on the stocks that interest you; it makes sense to use the services of a stockbroker certified to trade on the NSE, possesses superior knowledge of the market and can execute your buy or sell orders.

Brokers are the wonderful ladies and gentlemen on Broad Street and indeed around the world that act as middlemen between stocks traded on the NSE and investors like us that buy them. Just like any group of professionals, there are the good, the bad and definitely the ugly. If investing abroad is definitely new to you and the word Nigeria sounds like the scientific name of some chemical compound, selecting a good stockbroker may well be the most important action you could take before investing in Nigerian stocks. In 2002, a stockbroker working for a small securities company in Lagos called Bonkolans Investment Limited fraudulently sold shares in Nestle Nigeria belonging to some clients worth N314 million (about $2.5 million) in a bid to generate more commissions for his trading desk. Fortunately for the reputation of the market, investigators from the regulatory bodies discovered what happened and returned the monies to the victims. Unfortunately for the criminally-minded stock brokers, they are cooling their heels in prison; while the company has lost its reputation amongst investors.

If you trade in major markets in North America and Europe, it might not be shocking to you that securities fraud are usually committed by the individuals we expect and trust to invest our money for us without any qualms. However, many Nigerians were very surprised at the scale of the fraud because the mentality of the banking and investing public in Nigeria is that finance professionals hold themselves to a higher standard. Too bad, investors have to realize that some stockbrokers are more concerned about racking up commission revenues, rather than placing their clients' interest at the top of the list. For the most part, the fraud perpetuated by Bonkolans was more of the exception, than the rule.

STOCKBROKERS IN NIGERIA

In a world where the financial markets are fast becoming integrated and providing opportunities for people to invest in foreign equities, the biggest challenge has been how to conduct the actual trade. There are three options available to you if you seek to buy stocks in Nigeria. The first is purchasing individual stocks of foreign companies that are listed on the New York Stock Exchange as American Depositary Receipts (ADR), a convenient option for those of you who prefer trading strictly within the US, would rather have minimal contact with Nigerian financial advisors and do not want to be bothered with the issue of fluctuating exchange rates. The problem with going this route is that only one Nigerian company in 2006, the United Bank for Africa, was listed on the NYSE. This severely limits your selection of listed companies who have not jumped on the bandwagon of dual listing.

A second choice would be to invest in a mutual fund or Exchange Traded Fund (ETF) containing Nigerian stocks in its international portfolio. Such funds usually charge high transaction fees, charging a half-to-full percentage point in overhead costs above local transaction fees and some actively managed funds could cost you as much as three times the transaction cost of a local transaction. Again, just like the ADR option, the universe of Nigerian stocks covered in many of the Africa-focused funds offered by some Wall Street firms are so miniscule for you as an individual investor to participate fully and efficiently on the NSE. I have seen fund managers in New York select six stocks from thousands of listed companies in various African countries and called it an "African index fund". That is the worst description an educated fund manager can ever label a fund with only six stocks representing an entire continent!

The final option for you is to buy Nigerian stocks that are not available as ADRs but trade only on the NSE. This alternative offers you the widest access to company stocks, provides you with the most reliable market information and faster trades than going through a US or European based stockbroker. Using a local broker normally entails losing a percentage point or two to transaction costs due to currency exchange differences, bank transfer fees and different brokerage commissions based on the amount you are investing. To this end, I recommend using a local stockbroker as telecommunications and the internet have facilitated quick information transfers and sophisticated online trading. You can buy Nigerian stocks online using one of the biggest online trading firms in Africa, LiquidAfrica.com.

To engage in the trade of securities in the Nigerian stock market, interested individuals have to work for a stock broking company that is licensed to engage in that form of business. Additionally, all stock brokers in the country must pass professional examinations conducted by the Chartered Institute of Stockbrokers (CIS). Established in 1990, the CIS has the statutory role of regulating the stock broking practice in Nigeria; consistently evaluating the skill and knowledge of Nigerian brokers to be sure they are in sync with the regulations and laws in the securities industry. In the past, only Nigerian stockbrokers could trade on the NSE but with the deregulation of the financial services industry and increased foreign participation in the Nigerian economy; dealing licenses can be obtained by qualified brokers anywhere in the world. Many stockbrokers in Nigeria have had prior careers in the healthcare, accounting, banking, engineering, legal and other industries; making them very versatile when it comes to advising clients on the state of specific industries and companies. If you feel more comfortable dealing with a licensed broker in the US, ask your financial advisor or broker if they are licensed to trade Nigerian stocks and if not; try and get a recommendation from the NSE.

Although brokers have the primary job of trading stocks, they provide other services including advising you on what stocks to buy, writing investment research, selling financial products such as mutual funds, government and corporate bonds, foreign exchange; and conducting investment banking for companies that want to go public. Virtually all Nigerian stockbrokers provide these services mentioned in contrast to discount brokers (stock brokers who help you execute the trade without providing any advice or extra service) whom are gaining ground in the American stock market. The reason for this is that the majority of stock broking firms in the country are extensions of larger financial institutions such as the investment and commercial banks.

TYPES OF BROKERAGE ACCOUNTS

Most brokers in Nigeria offer investors the option of two trading accounts to facilitate stock trading. The first account is called a **Cash Account**, the traditional brokerage account where you deposit funds in a bank account of the broker's choice and instruct the broker to buy stocks with money in that account. If you decide to sell your stocks in a company, your broker would remit funds to your cash account. Many Nigerian banks would issue you a loan using your cash account as collateral. There is no minimum opening balance required for you to fund your cash account in Nigeria, as investors can get started with as little as $50 to open an account and commence trading. Compared to the normal $1,000 requirement of discount brokers in the United States and you will realize how affordable it could be to start trading in Nigerian stocks, even for a novice investor.

The second type of trading account brokers offer you in Nigeria is called a **Margin Account**. It is an improvement on the cash account as it allows you to take out loans based on the stocks you currently own. The extended credit is provided by your broker after they run a credit check on you and you sign a margin account agreement with the firm. If you are to trade on margin, you essentially and initially need to have a cash account. In Nigeria, the margin limit ranges from 30% to 50% but usually it is 50%, meaning that if you wanted to buy on margin $300,000 worth of stock in a company, you will require a minimum of $150,000 in your cash account before approaching your broker for extended credit to trade. If you have less than five years experience trading in any major stock market, I strongly suggest that you stick to trading Nigerian stocks using a cash account until you feel more comfortable with the economy and have garnered enough experience in timing the movement of particular stocks on the NSE. On the flip side, interest charges on margin accounts are really low; so if you score a winner with a good stock; you will have more than enough money to pay back your broker and have something to put in your piggy bank!

SETTING GOALS BEFORE TRADING

You probably know that stockbrokers make a lot of money from buying and selling stocks on behalf of their clients. Whether the customer makes money when prices jump sky-high or lose money in a bear market; brokers will always smile to the bank because the laws of finance dictate that they be paid a commission either way. Sounds rather unfair, but that is the way it is- deal with it. In such a scenario, it makes sense for many brokers to suggest that you buy this or sell that stock and it is so easy to forget the reason why you initially got into the stock market: to build wealth that could offer you a better way of living. It is so important for investors to remember this and not allow stockbrokers pitch them investments that have little relationship to their financial goals.

So the question is: what are your goals and how do you get a broker who is honest and responsible enough to work with you in developing an investing plan that can help you achieve those goals? Your answer depends on those three factors I mentioned earlier in Chapter 3: risk tolerance, age and income level. If you are a single lady in her mid-twenties making $85,000 a year, without a family to support and have a sizable capacity for risk; you might be interested in capital appreciation for your stock investments and might be a good fit with a broker who has the capability to make speculative and quick trades at the drop of a hat. Explaining your motives to your broker is very important so that your trades are made without him or her asking you what to do whenever a speculative trade opportunity comes by. If you are a 60 year old retiree receiving an annual pension payment of $25,000, seeking wealth preservation through a less aggressive style, so as to send your grandkids to college; you might focus on buying value stocks in corporations that have strong business fundamentals and are not easily prone to speculative trading. In this case, you will have minimal trades (as compared to a speculative investor) as you buy stocks that grow and provide steady returns over-time.

The stocks of these companies are generally divided into growth and income stocks. Growth stocks are characterized by earnings that are expected to grow at above-average rates relative to the general stock market. These kinds of stocks usually do not pay dividends as company management prefers to reinvest them into long-term capital projects. Income stocks on the other hand, focus on paying steady and increasing dividends to shareholders. With a lower level of volatility, income stocks are regarded as being less risky. A key thing to note while setting financial goals is the importance of involving you're a trusted family member or close friend that can discuss your financial plan with you and offer suggestions on how stock investing in Nigeria could be part of that financial plan. Getting a second opinion from this person could be vital if they have an unbiased approach to investing and can see through the sales pitch of a commission hungry broker and recognize an honest one. When you have gone about setting solid personal financial goals, join me and let's go shopping for a stockbroker!

SCREENING FOR A QUALITY STOCKBROKER

Apart from writing, I have been in the sales business since I was 14 years old and nothing gets my blood pumping as much as being able to provide a service that makes a client beam with satisfaction. One thing I realized while working for an internet start-up in Northern Virginia is that starting a business off the ground without customers who understand and know what your business is about can be challenging. To remedy the problem at this company, all the salespeople in the company engaged in aggressive 'cold calling', which involves calling people out of the blue with a pitch along the lines of their lives turning worthless if they do not buy our product! How do we know who to call? We used huge databases to screen millions of people across the country and select those people we believe have the big bucks to splurge on our services. The entire process is called prospecting. Almost all companies that cold-call you with cheesy sales pitches, use prospecting lists that identify you as such an individual.

Now that you are ready to buy stock in Nigerian companies, you must prospect for qualified brokers who have the capability of doing business with you; particularly since you live abroad. This part of the investing process should be exciting for you and excruciating for the broker- hey, they better sweat if they are going to manage your hard-earned money! It so reminds me of the nervous teenage boy who tries to ask the most beautiful girl in high school out on a date and she fires off fiery and unnerving questions that make him cringe in terror and forces incoherent mumbling from his mouth! That is exactly the way you should handle your stockbroker. No, I am not saying you should try to date your broker but it makes sense to ask the broker and yourself some critical questions if you want to build a professional, mutually beneficial and courteous relationship. Remember that you are not in the business of making friends with your broker; you are in this to make money. I have drawn up some questions that could guide your choice, here are some:

How experienced is the broker?

Your stockbroker should work for a brokerage that has been in business for more than a few days, say five years and beyond (although some brokerage firms in Nigeria are relatively young as a result of recent mergers, industry consolidations and entry of foreign brokers) before you consider them. Inquire on the size of assets managed by the firm to see if they have a large portfolio of client accounts under management. In Nigeria, $50 million should be a benchmark for your broker and they must have a fair mix of individual and institutional investors using their services. Also ask about the experience of the brokers and asset managers of the firm. What are their total years of experience in the market, do they have a track record of consistent performance in the Nigerian stock market and how many customer complaints have been brought against them by clients, if any? Are the brokers and analysts working for the firm registered with the appropriate agencies such as the Chartered Institute of Stockbrokers, Institute of Chartered Accountants, Nigerian Stock Exchange and the Securities Exchange Commission? What are their educational backgrounds? Do they deal with clients that reside in foreign countries and if so, how do they transact business with such clients?

What information do they provide?

Information is power and a lack of it may not be of any help to you investing in Nigerian stocks. Sure, there are a lot of newspapers and online resources that provide information on the economy and the stock market in general. Getting market information to clients live from the trading floor at the NSE is challenging but is usually accessible from most broker websites and the web portal of the NSE after trading ends. Sophisticated brokerage firms in the country normally provide news updates, research reports and other literature not easily accessible to investors outside Nigeria. I strongly suggest you choose a broker that publishes excellent research and disseminates them on time. On the subject of research, remember to be cautious about trading on insider information. If your relationship with a broker becomes strong enough to a point where he or she reveals insider information that you trade upon, you might be breaking the law and that may spell doom for you with the Nigerian SEC if you get caught. Be sure to keep your relationship with your broker professional and trade within the limits of the law, there is no amount of money worth breaking the law or going to jail for.

How effective are the communication channels?

The integration of technology and business in Nigeria is still low although there are exceptions to that rule in the financial services industry, particularly the banking and stock broking industries. Still, many brokerage firms do not offer real-time service such as online trading or live stock price updates such as that provided by Reuters Financial or Bloomberg for more advanced stock markets in the United States and Europe. At this time, if you think that is so "stone-ageist", I will not argue with you but say a lot of improvements are being made by some very innovative brokers. In such a situation, selecting a broker that keeps in touch regularly through phone calls and emails would be great. The majority of brokerage firms in Nigeria lack a strong customer-service orientation and many clients feel abandoned by their brokers. When prospecting for a broker, ask the company if you will be assigned an Account Officer who is dedicated to answering inquiries on your trading status and can provide you with vital information. The account officer is your go-to-guy when you want to retrieve your account statements or

CSCS report. Emphasize this point when interviewing brokers as some brokers do not have such officers (in a bid to cut on staffing costs) and will try to dodge the issue.

Can we talk about money?

There is no business that reminds people about the word 'commission' like the securities industry. Indeed, stockbrokers make a commission off of the amount an investor stakes in buying or selling stocks. At this stage in the interview, you must ask the broker how they are compensated. See, there are two ways brokers get compensated. The first is by commission only, where they get paid only when they an investor executes a trade through them. The other manner of compensation for brokers is a combination of an annual salary and commissions from trades, meaning they would still eat without your business.

From my experience investing both in the United States and Nigeria, it makes sense to use the second breed of brokers as they have less of an incentive to come up with reasons for you to trade constantly in order to generate more commissions. Most brokers in the country are full-service providers and make a lot more money from managing mutual funds and providing advisory services to high net worth and institutional clients. The other aspect of the money conversation should involve questions on transaction costs and how that affects the actual amount of money you invest and how much you get when you decide to sell. Trading commissions in Nigeria are relatively high (a $1,000 investment could cost you close to 3.9% in some instances, including money transfer charges which translates to $39 going to brokers and other financial intermediaries), so you have to weigh your options when it comes to the number and size of trades you will making; so you don't spend too much money making payments when you should be making money. Of course, transaction costs significantly go down the higher the amount of money invested and if you can negotiate effectively with the broker. This is business, every thing is negotiable. Top brokerage firms would charge you extra for premium services such as commissioned research, advice and facilitating huge trades (for example, if you wanted to go really big and buy a 5% stake in a company that really interests you). The fees might be pricey but worth it as returns in Nigeria have significantly outpaced trading costs, especially when you maintain a long-term investing perspective.

Are trades executed in accordance with client instructions?

It may amaze you to know that many stockbrokers across the world have become what I like to call "circumstantial lawyers", drawing unsuspecting investors into signing contracts that allow them make trades without prior assent by the investor. Before you sign and fax any paper work to a Nigerian broker, make sure you have your financial advisor or personal lawyer go over every inch of the business contract to be sure the broker is not given discretionary control over the account where the broker has the right to buy or sell stocks for you without your approval on every transaction. Even when you have built enough trust in your stockbroker, make sure you keep a close eye on your trading account statements. To avoid a situation where a broker trades your shares without prior authorization, you might want to sign up for an investor alert service offered by the CSCS. Called the Trade Alert System (TAS), it provides automatic notification over a mobile phone anytime there is activity on your account.

Some brokers would try to prevent you from selling a stock in which they have an interest and use every trick in the book to change your mind. If you have conducted adequate research on that particular company and feel it is time for you to sell, refuse to be intimidated by the convincing tone of the broker. In 2005, I made the decision to liquidate some shares in my portfolio account using the services of a leading brokerage in Lagos and was harangued by a senior official who called my decision to sell a "waste of time" and a hindrance to his sales target! If a broker uses a doomsday and arrogant attitude to coerce you into buying or selling a stock, change brokers fast like I did! Remember, you are the client, they need your business to remain in business and there are competing firms out there that will offer you better service if you demand it from them. If trades are conducted without your permission, contact the regulatory authorities immediately for redress.

There are over two hundred brokerages registered and licensed by the

SEC to conduct stock trading on the Nigerian stock exchange. With such a variety of firms, located in most major cities in the country; selecting a reputable broker could be quite a challenge. Since you live abroad, I will suggest you go on the internet and do a detailed search on stock broking firms in the country. Many brokerages in the country have websites with useful trading information and member-only sections where you access account information and trading tips. The internet provides some of the best information resource out there, usually providing updated content. You could also contact the Nigerian Embassy or Information service centers in Washington D.C. and New York, to provide you with relevant literature.

When you have combed through the list of stockbrokers, select a number of them and ask them the questions we discussed earlier. From my experience working on Broad Street, I have drawn up a list of reputable firms with their contact information in the appendix section of this book. Of course, the list is not by any means exhaustive but could be an effective guideline for you. The list does not serve as endorsement and I have received no compensation from the listed firms, but in my personal opinion, they are some of the innovative financial service firms in the country that have a track record of dealing with clients in the United States and Europe. Conduct your research on the many firms working on Broad Street, interview as many as possible and select one that you feel comfortable with.

As you select your stockbroker, I wish you a great business relationship and hope you send me letters chronicling your success investing in the Nigerian stock market. Maybe, someday; you will proudly introduce your Nigerian broker to me on your yacht!

Chapter 7
Managing the Nigerian Factor

Risk is a word many investors rather not hear. It seems to bear a foreboding element that makes you look not twice or thrice before you leap, but maybe never at all. In 2005, I delivered a presentation during an investment seminar to a bunch of Nigerians living in the United States about investing in Nigerian companies, explaining how market returns on the NSE had exceeded those of international stock markets and how to go about the whole process- basically what this book is doing for you. A friend of mine, an avid investor both in the Nigerian and American stock markets was taking notes and nodding his head, when from the corner of my eye I noticed a guy shaking his head almost in disbelief to what I was saying. During question time, he stood up and didn't ask a question but decided to comment on my presentation. He then proceeded to explain that Nigeria was a dangerous country where investing was a no-no and advised the group to stay out of the Nigerian stock market. Talk about being embarrassed! I calmly asked him what the basis for his assertion was and his evidence were the many news reports on the internet and television news channels that depicted Nigeria as a nation full of corrupt individuals out to swindle every single dollar from foreigners. Someone in the crowd even suggested that there might be a civil war in the country, which stunned many Nigerians who did not understand why some in the crowd had such a pessimistic view of their country. Need a simple answer? The sensationalist views of the Western media to most things that occur in Africa. However, the truth be told; there are always two sides to a coin and some of the comments on the situation in Nigeria do hold water.

Nigerians are very proud of their heritage and despite the turbulence the country has experienced over the second half of the 20th century, they have managed to institute democracy in the polity, build billion-dollar businesses, create a highly skilled workforce and sustain their entrepreneurial traits from street corners to the boardroom, not only in the country but around the world. It all sounds colorful and rosy looking at the country from that perspective, except for the fact that the country has a dark side that has caused it to be portrayed so negatively in the Western media. It is easy to understand the faulty portrayal of the country when Transparency International, the international N.G.O. that monitors accountability and governance in countries around the world ranks Nigeria as one of the most corrupt nations on the planet. Maybe those famous scam letters you find in your email box inviting you to participate in some dubious business transaction that can make you a millionaire just by providing your personal and banking information, while sending a couple of hundreds to complete the deal, do not help any P.R. effort by the government. A failed history of political leadership under brutal military dictatorships, a large number of the population living below the poverty line although the country has earned over $300 billion in the last forty years, criminal attacks in major cities, religious and ethnic tensions periodically flaring up and the presence of fraud in many economic sectors, are just the kinds of stories that would scare any investor away from this emerging market.

Humorous as ever no matter their plight, Nigerians have coined a phrase to capture these problems that afflict their country. They call it the "Nigerian Factor". It is not uncommon to hear a Nigerian businessman joking about not getting a government contract because of his ethnic background or decision not to pay a bribe to a corrupt government official, blaming it on the "Nigerian Factor". When you start investing in the country, factor this factor into your equation. Although I am very proud of my country, the reality is that these things do happen and would take time to abate; no matter how committed successive administrations try to tackle the matter. Don't get me wrong, things are changing faster than imagined but real change in every facet of the Nigerian society that would place the country on par with the democracies of the United States and Europe would probably start to take hold in the next 30 to 50 years.

Am I trying to dissuade you from buying Nigerian stocks after giving you valid and tangible reasons why you should? No. All I hope to do is to provide a balanced overview of the investing climate in Nigeria and inform you on the risk factors you should consider when investing there. The maxim goes "High Risk, High Return" and no other country embodies that statement more than Nigeria. It is a resource abundant nation that has expanded its economy but still struggles with the ilk of so-called Third World nations. It is an investors delight due to the size of its population that is a ready market for virtually sorts of goods and services. Many have made millions of dollars investing in Nigeria and they did so by mitigating the impact the Nigerian Factor would have on their investments. In this chapter, you will be introduced to the types of risk that exist in Nigeria and that can impact your stock investments; and the fraudulent practices that any cautious investor should be well informed on.

UNDERSTANDING INVESTMENT RISK IN NIGERIA

Risk is an ever present phenomenon that surrounds us and we all deal with in our own special ways. As I stated earlier, investing in Nigeria could be considered risky for some, for me and others who have made a decent amount of money in the Nigerian stock market; it is not since we operate on facts and not fiction based on news reports and generalizations of global financial analysts that have never set foot in Africa, talk less of Nigeria and monitoring how commerce works there. Risk is relative and depends on your perspective and capability to manage it effectively. For example, Nigeria's largest city of Lagos with almost 16 million residents in the metropolitan area is considered a dangerous place to live in by the rest of the country, although it records less murders and carjacking than what obtains in the cities of Los Angeles, Atlanta or Houston in the United States. In fact, you are 15 more times likely to be involved in a gunshot or robbery incident in New York than in Lagos. The challenge for you if and when you invest in Nigeria is to be confident in the individuals you would be working with in managing your investments, keep a critical eye on all facets of the investment process and view the country from an unbiased business standpoint as an emerging market where you could become a leading investment pioneer in the near future.

Remember Germany after World War II, South Korea after the 1957 war, South Africa after decades of apartheid government and Ireland that was bedeviled by sectarian violence? These countries were considered "HIGHLY RISKY" during those periods and have emerged as leading industrialized nations that dominate the global economy. If you had bought stock in companies in those countries at the early phases of their economic turn-around programs, you will be very rich without a doubt and very old today because it's been a little while! Nigeria is at a very interesting phase in its economic life and if there is a better time to get in and make some real money in that country, the time is now.

The political situation since 1999 has been stable and Nigeria has experienced the longest period of democratic rule, with the Obasanjo Administration being the most committed government to implementing economic and political reform in the country. This political will, though with its hiccups, gave room to unprecedented economic growth in Nigeria, with annual GDP averaging 5.6% in the years 1999 through 2005. The once moribund telecom industry that international investors shied away from has become the fastest growing telecom market in the world, growing from a $200 million sector into a $25 billion industry in just five years. For the first time in 2006, the country received BB sovereign ratings from agencies such as Fitch Incorporated and Standard and Poor's, elevating its investment profile from the rankings of Iran and Bangladesh and placed it in the same investment class as Brazil, Turkey and South Africa.

The regulatory environment has improved with the National Assembly (the equivalent of the US Congress) passing legislation aimed at good governance, accountability and transparency in both the private and public sectors; guaranteeing the safety of the investments of domestic and foreign investors. The investment opportunities outside the Nigerian stock market are enormous and attracting investments from global energy, telecom, service and technology companies; creating jobs and initiating an economic revolution that the country has never experienced since the discovery of oil in 1958. If you can 'see' what I am saying and still have some serious concerns about investing in Nigeria, I suggest you stay away from the Nigerian stock market until you gather more information on the subject, do your research and feel you are ready to invest. Hopefully, you don't get in late like investors who are just now investing in "matured" markets such as the NYSE, Toronto Stock Exchange or Frankfurt. Despite the fact that investing in Nigeria and its stock market could be a lucrative venture for savvy investors, there is always some form of risk just like in any other market.

TYPES OF RISK

There are many forms of risk that relate to investing in general and others that are stock-specific. They include interest rate risk, socio-economic risk, market risk, tax-related risk and so many others with even snazzier names that business theorists seem to churn almost on a daily basis. If you are buying Nigerian stocks, here are some you should have at the back of your mind:

Socio-political Risk

As mentioned in Chapter 1, Nigeria has over 250 ethnic groups that all desire to gain political power at the Federal level that grants any political grouping control over the huge resources scattered across the country; particularly oil and gas. The presence of these ethnic differences, coupled with the ever recurring religious conflicts between the predominantly Muslim northern part of the country and the Christian southern, has intensified under democratic rule unlike in the past where the military quickly suppressed dissent and used brutal force to quell such demonstrations. The 1999 and 2003 democratic elections were considered "fair" by international observers and Nigeria has experienced the longest period of stability in its history. The best part of the Obasanjo administration was its consistency in policy formulation and implementation, which provided a sense of normality and structure in key economic sectors as exhibited by the deregulation of the downstream sector of the oil industry and privatization of government-owned enterprises.

Investing in a company that is affected by government policies that change so often could definitely be a gamble for you, especially if other investors decide to abandon the stock (rightly so) for a more stable stock. In the 1980s, the military government allowed massive importation of textiles from Asian and European countries, which often sold for ridiculously low prices. When different administrations came along, they offered new incentives for domestic production of textile and imposed tariffs on some textile imports. For a little while, it worked but then powerful import lobbies managed to get the revised trade policy reversed. This inconsistency reduced domestic production capacity in the textile industry to as low as 15% in 2002, causing thousands of textile workers to lose their jobs and investors abandon textile stocks on the NSE.

Also, social unrest has developed from a rare occurrence to a periodic militant nuisance in the oil-rich Niger Delta region of the country. With over 85% of Nigeria's oil resources produced in this region, cases of kidnapping and pipeline sabotaging affects world markets; since Nigeria is the eight largest producer of oil in the world and accounts for 9% of US oil imports. Local oil companies listed on the NSE whose core business is the marketing and distribution of oil in the West African sub region, could have their revenue forecasts severely impeded if the production and transportation of gas products is stopped. You can minimize the impact of political and social risk by watching news events in the country and requesting periodic reports from your financial advisor or stockbroker in Nigeria.

Currency Risk

Nigeria operates a deregulated foreign exchange system, meaning the government does not impose controls on the movement of the national currency, the Naira. Leaving market forces to determine the value of the Naira in comparison to the dollar guarantees fluctuations in the exchange rate overtime. Since you live abroad and would be sending dollars to your broker to buy stocks in the local currency, currency risk is a concept that should be monitored closely. To better understand the downside of foreign exchange and its impact on your stock investments, you must understand how the appreciation or depreciation of the dollar affects the value of your investment. If you commit $5,000 to buying stock in Texaco Nigeria and the local currency goes for N150/$1 at the time, the value of your investment, ignoring transaction costs and other charges for a moment, would be equal to N750, 000. If the dollar appreciates against the naira by N20 (which means the naira trades at N170 now for a dollar), your investment would have lost $588 because now; it would take only $4,411 to buy the same N750, 000 worth of Texaco Nigeria. If the naira gains N20 against the dollar, your $5,000 now in dollar terms would have increased to $5,769 if you were to sell them and convert them back to US dollars. This is an interesting point because if the naira gains against the dollar continuously and the company you invested in makes significant capital gains and pays decent dividends, you should make a handsome profit.

Now let's go back to the subject of risk, it's always exciting to jog your memory with a little math! Realize that Nigeria's economy is tied significantly to its oil sector which is the largest source (about 85%) of its foreign exchange receipts. In a situation of global oil prices rising rapidly, Nigeria like any oil-rich nation, tends to build a substantial foreign exchange reserve which traditionally precipitates the strengthening of its currency against major currencies like the dollar. If that happens, the value of your stock investments would go up and you should have a huge smile on your face. If the reverse happens, due to the mismanagement of foreign reserves on massive importation which the Nigerian economy and society is prone to, the inherent currency risk should be factored into your decision.

Financial Risk

This type of risk occurs when a company does not have enough cash in the bank to cover its financial obligations, both short and long-term. If the company cannot meet those obligations such as pay its workers on time, buy the necessary equipment to boost production, invest in plant expansion and do the important things that make the business grow and profitable; it faces severe financial risk and is likely to go bankrupt. This is why it is so vital for you to do your research before buying stocks in Nigeria or anywhere else for that matter. Many companies across the world use very creative accounting techniques to hide their poor financial conditions. One of the biggest sources of financial risk for companies is the mismanagement of company debt. Most companies finance their operations with a combination of equity (stocks) and debt such as corporate bonds and loans sourced from banks. The problem with debt is that if the management do not plough those borrowed funds into projects that will generate more revenue for the company, company expenses may explode out of control and the company's financial managers would have to refinance those loans- basically borrowing more money to pay off past loans! Such companies have bad omens and should be avoided.

A good way to minimize this risk pattern is to look for companies that have healthy cash flows; this eliminates half of the task when doing your research. In Nigeria, there are some companies that have liquidity problems that are the basis for their crumbling businesses. Their poor state of affairs may force them to engage in very creative accounting which your accountant should be able to spot after going through their balance sheets. Some are even so desperate as to solicit unscrupulous financial journalists to give them good reviews in the media. Do not allow analysts, brokers and news sources; be the only guiding lights to avoid financial risk. Do your research and consult independent analysts that can verify certain information and recommend the stocks that have minimal financial risk inherent to their operations. Since 2002, the Nigerian economy has improved remarkably and the nation's capital markets have been doing brisk business- raising billions of dollars for companies to expand their operations. Many Nigerian banks and oil companies are growing so fast and even spreading their operations past the West African sub region into other parts of Africa. Stock prices of companies in that category have cumulatively gained more than 600% between 2003 and the mid-2006. Talk about making some serious cash!

However, as the informed and cautious investor I believe you ought to be, there is still that element of financial risk. Conduct your research, plan diligently and do not fall prey to the exuberance of the financial media and analysts. See through it all and focus only on winning stocks.

DIVERSIFICATION: The key to managing your risk exposure

You probably have heard someone say "you have to diversify your portfolio to minimize your risk", nodded your head in agreement and went home scratching your head trying to figure out what that meant. In the financial world, the technical definition of diversification is a risk management method that involves the combination of different types of investments within an individual or institutional portfolio; with the aim of lowering risk and averaging higher returns on the total investment portfolio. If you are like me, you would prefer the layman definition: do not place all your eggs in one basket.

One of the greatest banes of many individual investors is that they have too much stake in a particular stock or industry. I know of investors who would buy nothing other than banking stocks. When I ask them why, they proudly tell me that banks deal with money, know how to manage and make it and should be every investor's first pick when selecting stocks. Now if that is not a simplistic and stupid logic to investing, I don't what is! We live in a world where things change rapidly and if your "loyalty" to a stock is your only reason for investing, you are in for a big shock when sweeping change affects your portfolio. For example, the Nigerian telecom industry is one of the fastest growing in the world. Now imagine some operators in the industry head to the stock market for equity financing. Investing in those companies would be a smart choice as the industry has a huge growth potential and attracts huge foreign investments. If you commit your entire portfolio holdings to telecom stocks, it could be a profitable venture but not a smart action in the event something affects that industry. Suppose the Nigerian government removes industry and price-setting barriers that are characteristic of telecom markets around the world and huge phone companies across the world invade the Nigerian telecom market, the intense competitive environment would cause prices to crash and the revenues of most telecom firms would probably stay flat.

Now you know for a fact that we are in this together to make money, not invest in companies with flat revenues; so you might regret sticking to a single industry. If you are a veteran investor, you should know the full benefits of diversification can not be underestimated especially when investing in stocks and other assets. Investing abroad is an exciting adventure for maverick investors and those who seek value outside their comfort zones; and want to build an income stream outside their home countries. Diversification in foreign stocks, particularly Nigerian stocks, could be a lucrative alternative since there is a lower correlation with domestic stocks in the US. Diversification is an option that you should consider when you start investing. Let me suggest some tips on doing just that when you start investing in Nigeria:

Don't place your eggs....

Yes, that maxim is so valid when talking about diversification. The odds are against you if you think that investing in one stock would make you an overnight millionaire. It makes sense to spread your portfolio funds across a wider spectrum to minimize your risk. So if you have $10,000 that you want to invest with, buy stocks in different companies and industries; that way, the risk would be greatly reduced and you won't have bouts of anxiety worrying about what happens to a SINGLE company. Become your own financial analyst and select stocks in companies and industries that have solid business fundamentals, offer goods and services with strong and growing demand and stable management. A good way to look for such companies is to focus on those that offer essential services such as utilities, real estate and food. Come on, how many food companies out there are doing badly? If we don't eat, we can't invest right? I think I just hinted on what companies in Nigeria that could be of interest to you!

Buy Mutual Funds

Now if you are an institutional investor with billions of dollars in the bank to buy virtually every stock on the NSE, you would be well diversified but for the individual investor, that is not usually an option. The answer to the dilemma for the small investor is to invest in a mutual fund. Mutual funds are pools of stocks where the manager of the fund brings a large number of small investors together and invests their money in stocks, bonds and other securities. If you become an investor in a mutual fund, you become a shareholder in the fund and are issued shares in the same manner shares are issued to you if you were investing in a single company listed on the stock exchange. The beauty of mutual funds is that you become a shareholder in more companies than you can afford if you invested on your own.

Most Nigerian brokerages and investment banks offer mutual funds that vary depending on your investing style, religious or moral beliefs and sectors; so be sure to inquire on the mutual fund products that they may offer. As a first priority, select a no-load mutual fund (a fund that does not charge you a fee when you invest) if your broker offers that alternative. In Nigeria, try and save your investment funds for investing and avoid high transaction costs that you could incur by buying a load fund that requires a fee upfront (usually a percentage of your total investment) before investing. Apart from diversification, a major benefit of mutual funds is that they are managed by professional fund managers; usually a track record of superior performance in investing. Mutual fund fees are usually cheaper than commissions charged by stockbrokers so that saves you a significant amount of money that could be invested elsewhere.

Invest in Money Market Funds

These are similar to mutual funds only that their managers are called money managers and they invest strictly in money market instruments. If you are risk averse and feel some stocks might be too volatile for you to stomach, you could request your broker to sell some of your stock holdings and place the funds into a money fund.

These alternative funds resemble a special savings account, and unlike mutual funds that invest in stocks; money managers buy investments which include fixed-income securities such as bonds, treasury bills and certificates. Although, they tend to invest in financial instruments that are safer than stocks; returns on these funds are not guaranteed despite the fact they are less risky. The good thing about money market funds is that they rarely lose money because the underlying investments are usually issued by the government and large corporations, which carry a comparatively low rate of risk.

419: AVOIDING THE CON MEN

Just as the Mafia remains a deep part of Italian society and makes the world look at the town of Sicily more as a den of murderers and drug peddlers than the beautiful countryside spectacle that it is, Nigeria's Achilles heel is its infamous Advanced Fee Fraud syndrome- an elaborate scam perpetuated by Nigerian criminals but gaining popularity around the world, that convinces individuals around the world to send relatively small amounts of money as payment for a larger cash sum. Popularly called the "419" scheme, aptly named after Section 419 of the Nigerian penal code dealing with cases of fraudulent activity; advanced fee fraud more than government corruption is the greatest turn-off for foreign investors seeking opportunity in Nigeria.

In the past, it was carried out by a few fraudsters who used fax machines and traditional snail mail to entrap greedy foreigners seeking to make a fast buck in a foreign country, even though all the red flags screamed SCAM! Today, with advanced data mining software and the proliferation of internet cafes on almost every street corner in Nigerian cities, the industry has thousands of unemployed men, even teenagers, sending emails around the globe and scamming an estimated $2 billion annually from foreigners. Some analysts have gone as far as saying that the 419 industry is Nigeria's third largest foreign exchange earner after oil and cocoa. Located in the inner districts of major Nigerian cities like Lagos, Port-Harcourt and Aba; these scam artists called *Yahoo Boys* send millions of spam email daily to people around the world with a simple but fleecing pitch. A common pitch used by the scammers goes a little like this: They represent a wealthy Nigerian or family of a dead ex-military ruler who seeks to transfer vast sums of money (usually millions of dollars) out of the country due to persecution and surveillance from the Nigerian government and need your assistance in facilitating the money transfer. For your help, you will be offered between 15 and 40% of the money to be transferred. Once the email recipient agrees to the 'deal', the scammers would request proof of identification such as your banking information and other documents. Once the fraudsters are confident that the victim is so attuned to the thought of making "easy money", they will inform him that everything is in place and that all that is needed is a spurious transfer fee or government tax to be paid.

On receipt of the first payment, the scammers would send fake documents bearing official government and bank documents, certificates, seals and stamps; to gain the victim's trust. With trust gained, they start creating excuses for the delay in effecting the transaction; boldly asking for extra payments to close the deal. Excuses range from the need to bribe a government official to processing fees for "special" documents, all the while, promising the gullible victim that the deal is just about to be closed. After the victim realizes what has happened to them, the scam artist ends all form of communication and in a cyber world where anonymity can be common currency, disappears into thin air. Many people seek redress, few do while many never file a report with the authorities because of the embarrassment they anticipate from family, business partners, coworkers (it sure would be embarrassing for your coworkers to realize you fell for such a stupid scam, I know I would) and the authorities

As the Nigerian economy blossoms and the stock market gains increasing reputation with foreign investors, I predict that criminals would invade cyberspace with creative scams to fleece prospective investors. I happen not to have a criminal mind and cannot forecast what the details of potential 419 schemes would be but I do know, it would be related to the stock market and could cause investors to lose a lot of money if they allow their gullibility get the best of them.

Now I know that some persons after reading a less than inspiring chapter on risk and fraud in Nigeria would say, "Hey, there is no way I am going to invest my money in Nigerian stocks or any other venture after reading something like this". If you feel that way, well don't invest. Investing abroad does not need a negative attitude. It demands an intelligent and well informed perspective, the hallmark of smart investors. If you never knew about this scam before reading this book, now you can identify such risks and avoid them. The 419 syndrome is one of them and should not scare you. It all boils down to being able to the identification and elimination of risk in the investing process.

Remember that risk is an ever-present phenomenon in every country, including the one you are in right now while reading this book. Even the United States has a huge problem with scam artists on Wall Street, particularly the classic "boiler room" scam. In these boiler rooms, dishonest brokers cold-call prospective investors and try to sell them so-called "house stock" (stocks in little known companies that the brokerage has a huge stake in), so as to beef up the price in the stock market. Once the stocks have reached a target price level, these brokers then commence selling off THEIR stockholdings and leave their victims with a stock that quickly loses its value and usually gets delisted by the stock exchange pretty soon. That is an example of risk and fraud not found in Nigeria (well, not yet!).

Avoid scammers and report your case to the relevant authorities if you feel you have been scammed or if you are not comfortable going forward with an investment, either in stocks or any other venture. Contact the Nigerian law enforcement authorities through the Nigerian Embassy in Washington D.C. or any consulate office in the city nearest to you. They would put you in touch with the SEC, NSE and CSCS and the financial crimes monitoring agency in Nigeria, the Economic and Financial Crimes Commission. You could also contact the United States Secret Service's criminal division for advice on your case. The contact information for all these agencies is provided in the appendix section. At this juncture, allow me reiterate the importance of having a good broker. Many of you would find out that your broker in Nigeria would become your financial advisor, analyst and a vital source of information on other investment matters. They understand the Nigerian economy well enough to spot a scam and could be a life saver, when you least expect it. Now that you have a better understanding of risk in Nigeria, go ahead and strategize on the best manner in which to start investing in the most exciting economy on the African continent.

Chapter 8
Survival Tips for Investors

Every time you invest in some asset, whether it be real estate, stocks or some other venture; the feeling you get when that investment pays off is undeniably awesome. That kind of feeling first overwhelmed me when I started selling paintings as an undergraduate student at the University of Ilorin in Nigeria. I was a broke 19 year-old just scraping off a much needed monthly allowance from my parents and profiting from the small business deals my elder sister and I conducted through my mother's catering business on the university campus. However, there always seemed not to be enough despite the fact I was a prudent spender (far from being an investor). Around the period, I had made a rather painful and foolish decision to drive one of my father's vehicles on the condition that I gas it at my own expense; an action that drained even more of my little savings as gas was quite expensive for the average Nigerian consumer. When I thought things could not get worse, I fell in love with a girl who one day realized that my sweet words were not substitute for the traditional gifts that she liked! As far as I was concerned, my financial situation was at an all-time low and could not get any lower.

Around the time, I came in contact with a classmate's brother who happened to be a painter, negotiated a reseller contract with him and sold reproduced copies of his paintings at a 150% price mark-up. Needless to say, business was brisk and life was all good. My painter friend probably after finding out that I was making a killing on his paintings, upped his selling price and our once solid (though financially lopsided) business relationship tanked and I found another venture to sustain myself for the rest of my college life. I guess he was worth his price as he has since gone on to become an internationally renowned painter with his works adorning the entrance of the World Bank building in Washington D.C.

As I have matured in the business world and investing has allegedly become my forte, I have ventured into various business projects with varying end results. Along the way, I have made a lot of mistakes, made some money and learnt valuable lessons from more experienced investors. In this chapter, I will share some of the lessons that would help you while investing in Nigerian stocks. Some of them are well known and sound so clichéd but may be helpful both for the veteran and novice crowds, either way, they are important nuggets of wisdom that could make the difference between losing and making money in the Nigerian market.

Thrive on fact, not fiction

The mere fact that this book is in your hands is proof that you seek more than the surface information on foreign equities that many US based investors are scammed into thinking is the gospel truth. In the 21st century, the Nigerian economy is positioned to become one of the most important financial markets in the world; considering its huge population, vast natural resources and prominent position as a sub-regional superpower. True enough, there would be lapses here and there (that is the undeniable phenomena of risk at work) but if current political and economic conditions remain steady or improve, the country is sure to experience the sort of economic revolution that the Asian Tigers underwent between the late 1970's and 2000. However, some of the news reported by global media corporations seems to be constantly negative and could scare any investor from participating in one of the biggest financial revolutions occurring on the African continent.

One of the biggest disservices to the image of Nigeria has been the reports on security and crime in the country that have been blown out of proportion, traditionally by the Western media. Do not be shocked to believe that many Nigerians are as shocked as foreigners when false media reports are made on international news networks like the popular case in 2004, when a CNN correspondent wrongly attributed chaos in a highbrow area of Lagos to calls from the public for a return to military rule; while in actual fact, the ruckus was caused by thousands of people escaping violent explosions from an abandoned military depot containing expired and apparently unsafe artillery bombs. True enough, there are pockets of criminal activity and political instability that scare even me from undertaking certain investments; however, it should be taken into context. A few years ago, a British friend of mine who has a penchant for traveling to all places alien and dangerous expressed his disappointment at the relative calm he experienced during visits to Lagos and Ibadan; telling me his parents wept watching him board the plane at Heathrow airport!

The intent for the unusually negative portrayal of the country in the media could be debated but is not the reason why you bought this book, however, it should not be a deterrent to your considering Nigerian stocks as an investment option. The millions of investors, foreign and domestic, trading stocks in Nigerian companies are not scared of the market and are proof that there exists a viable investment opportunity for you abroad. To clear the cloud of misinformation, do not take my word for it but make a commitment to learn more about Nigeria, its politics, economy and every other thing there is to know. This book will not do that for you but there are hundreds of Nigerian newspapers, many with websites and other resources easily accessible over the internet that will broaden your knowledge of the country. In my opinion, I suggest you get a Nigerian friend. Nigerians love to talk and are not very sophisticated at embellishing the truth about what goes on in their country. Putting the country and what goes on inside it into perspective is the key to investing successfully abroad. While others run scared based on what they 'heard', you can act based on what you 'know'.

Determine if you are an investor or speculator

Investors are interested in the long term potential of a company and invest with the plan that the stock moves in tandem with the growth potential of the company itself. Successful speculators like Warren Buffet have a ten year horizon for companies that they invest in, emphasizing that steady long term revenue and earnings growth is better than staking their money on the chance making sporadic profits. Speculators on the other hand are short term oriented seeking to make a buck whenever arbitrage opportunities present themselves, exactly what stockbrokers do because it helps them generate more commissions and can provide substantial gains.

Speculative investing is definitely riskier than taking a long-term investing approach but many investors have made money going this way. I do not have an opinion on which method is better as I believe individual personality drives individual investing strategies; all I suggest is that you do your research and avoid letting greed get in the way of rationality. However, I must point out that Nigerian companies are not 'ripe' for the kind of speculation that drives many stocks in US markets. The majority of investors in the Nigerian stock market are long-term investors, possibly because of the cultural aversion amongst Nigerians to simultaneous buying and selling. In Nigeria, it is estimated that less than 40% of market capitalization is actually traded due to the buy and hold attitude of Nigerians and for some uncanny reason, foreign investors in the market follow the same trend.

I guess I can safely say that beating the market with a maverick speculative style would not do well except you have the deep pockets to actually make block trades in specific companies that are sensitive to government policies or sudden changes in economic trends. As I stated earlier in the book, whatever plan you decide to go along with; make sure you remain committed to it and avoid the tendency to digress at the instance of shaky market conditions. The emergence of large capital movement from the international community into the Nigerian economy and its capital markets could and probably will shift the focus of the market from an investor's market to a speculative one someday. For those of you who have the patience and tenacity to override short-term fluctuations in the market, taking a long-term approach to investing in the market seems like a logical and oftentimes, profitable move. I still believe being a long-term investor is the number one way to override temporary downturns in the market and minimize your overall risk, especially currency risk, since every time you exchange dollars for naira; there is some loss in value and more transaction costs that eat into your profit. Which ever way the market moves, exercise some flexibility when making your investment decision so as not to miss out on trading opportunities.

Be comfortable making a loss

One of my favorite jokes about stock investing is the one where a college student about to graduate, seeks the advice of this financial whiz kid in his dormitory room who seems to constantly have research reports strewn on the floor and huge charts of stock movements on his wall. He asks the kid "How much do I need to invest in the stock market to have a million dollars in the next 12 months?" The smart kid looks up to the ceiling, ponders in thought for a minute and finally answers "Start with two million dollars!" Now that may not make you smile if you are new to investing but I can guarantee that the stock market is one place that teaches you how to both lose and win, depending on if you ignore or adhere to sound investing principles.

Although studies have always shown that stock markets overtime generate returns that exceed those of 'safer' investments such as government bonds and real estate, many people avoid them because they are scared silly of losing any money. Some stocks on the NSE will tank, that is a given despite the fact that the market has had more winners than losers over the years. If you do incur some losses, it could be a call to run for the hills but doing so could deny you of other winners in the market. In this instance, educate yourself some more on investing and discuss with your financial advisor on how best to pick winners. If you are the investor who sells a stock once it starts losing value all the time, I do not think the stock market is for you. To the best of my knowledge, no investor has made a fortune by panicking after making a loss. Remember the mantra: high risk, return. If you factor that into your investment psyche, losing money on a trade would be an indicator that you should do more research and draw up a winning strategy for the future. The key to not running out of your mind when you see a stock's value go down, down and down is to cut your losses when you can. If a stock loses 4% in a day, 5% the next day, 12% down the third day; I guess my question is: WHAT IN THE WORLD ARE YOU WAITING FOR?!

I am a simple investor and personally believe you should sell a stock that loses 15% of its value in a trading week. After conducting your analysis and find that it still has strong fundamentals; once its price starts recovering, go ahead and buy. I don't think there is any justification for losing value in the name of investor loyalty or company management sweet talking you into backing a horse that is obviously not riding in the right direction. At the same time, do not get so emotionally tied up in the investment that you break down when the stock tanks. After all, there are some good buying opportunities when stock prices crash. Many financial experts would tell you that a down market is usually the best time for you to buy stocks since they come on the block for cheap. In all my years of investing, I still follow a simple rule: buy low, sell high and don't cry over split milk. Pick yourself up, strategize and live to fight and profit another day!

Take baby steps

Although there is money to be made in stocks, I cringe in fear whenever I see an overzealous investor willing to stake it all just become he saw or heard about some guy who makes a million a day by being "aggressive" and "risky" in the stock market. I remember a particular day when a friend of mine who happened to have a lot of free cash on him ($20,000 idling away while in college was a big deal to me and should be to you, if you are thinking of writing that term paper after reading this book) called me and asked for my advice on which banking stocks to invest in Nigeria. I calmly told him to invest only $2,000 since he had never invested in the market and I needed him to gain some practical experience before committing larger funds. He was especially disappointed by my recommendation as he saw the huge gains the banking sector was racking up and wondered why I will suggest such a passive move.

The truth is that winners in the stock market are usually those who understand the value patience can generate for their portfolios. Whether you are a first-timer or experienced investor, the best investment opportunities are reserved for the patient and disciplined. When growing up, I remember my father admonishing me (especially with all my business ventures that kept crumbling because I moved too fast) that "there is no rush in making money, it would find you if you sit still". Investing in a foreign market can be a tricky dance requiring stringent research and a whole lot of patience. My suggestion to you is to invest about 30% of the funds you have available to invest in Nigerian stocks, wait between six and nine months to determine your comfort level in the NSE and then decide after this review period, if more funds should be committed to your Nigerian stock portfolio. While researching for this book, a lot of persons interested in the Nigerian stock market expressed their concerns of investing in companies that they have never heard of.

In that case, you could start and play it safe by investing in American and European multinationals that have huge operations in Nigeria such as Texaco, Nestle, Dunlop, Mobil, Guinness, Cadbury, Longman Publishing and others. There are other Nigerian companies that your stockbroker can furnish you with more details. As you mature in this market through patient investing, you will avoid the many mistakes anxious and impatient investors normally make around the world and everyday.

Buy the good stuff

Would you go to the grocery store, pick up a bottle of milk that expired three days ago and rationalize your purchase on the basis that a few days really does not constitute a health risk? If your answer is yes, you should be punished for such naïve thinking and undergo a thorough physical examination! As we discussed earlier, when you approach the stock market; you are not merely buying stocks but buying part of a larger company. Therefore, it makes sense for you to buy companies with excellent financials, solid business operations – by that I mean providing a service or product that has steady demand and good management. On the NSE, like in any other stock market, there are some terrible companies that are listed for the pride of being referred to as a publicly quoted company but obviously lack the characteristics of investment-worthy companies. However, there are still millions of investors around the world that pour billions of dollars into companies because some broker or analyst called it the next "big thing", whatever that means.

If you are just investing for the first time and not ready to plunge into some of the little unknowns on the NSE, start with the blue-chip firms. Why should you start with these? Because they are the most prosperous, progressive and oftentimes largest companies in the stock market run by some of the best managers that money can buy. The blue chip companies in Nigeria are concentrated in the food, banking, conglomerate, brewery, petroleum marketing and real estate sectors on the NSE. These companies normally have well known products, sophisticated distribution channels, large sales armies and export their products to the neighboring countries in West and Central Africa; guaranteeing an ever growing target market. Now that is all well and good for the company but you ask, "what is in it for me?" Well, blue chip firms in Nigeria have a steady and long history of profitability and paying higher dividends, in comparison to second tier companies; and normally weather the tough times when the economy experiences a downturn.

I have been accused of being a blue-chip stalwart but on the contrary; I have invested in smaller companies. However, my advice to people who have never invested abroad is to always start with the well-known blue chips; then after gaining some experience investing those companies, proceed to explore growth stocks in the small cap market. I strongly believe this is a vital risk management perspective especially if you are risk averse to emerging markets. Sure enough there are smaller companies listed on the second-tier market that are properly managed and have strong business models but your investment in such companies should only be transacted after due consultations with local brokers and your personal financial advisor.

Take Charge!

Too many investors out there believe that the market has enough people "watching over" their investments like angels hanging over a pile of stock certificates. With analysts constantly reviewing stock performance, economists telling us how the economy is doing, regulators threatening to bring down firms that violate investor confidence, brokers giving us 'guaranteed tips' to make us tons of money and politicians introducing tough legislation overseeing the financial markets; it is so easy to believe that Broad Street is so effectively looking out for your best interest. Think so? Yes? *Ngggghhhhhh......*wrong answer!!! No one looks out for you in the financial world better than yourself; you know your financial goals, understand what makes you feel comfortable in a broker and should have the final say on an investment decision.

Starting from the time a company crosses your radar, I want you to roll up your sleeves and start researching that company to the best of your ability. Check out online news reports on the company, study its industry and then call your broker or buy a research report for further information. After that is all and done, decide whether you want to buy or sell the stock. Many investors leave this initial step in the hands of the 'experts' when a little research on their part would put them in the same league. As the eccentric financial guru Jim Cramer would say: "Tips are for waiters", so don't let some fast talking broker sweet talk you into buying stocks you have not taken the time to study personally. I am not a trained financial analyst (although having an MBA does not hurt) and I can tell you that analyzing companies takes plain common sense and some few hours a week studying the companies that interest you. Let the buying decision be yours and not solely that of the experts; trust me, if not for any other thing, do it for self pride!

The next thing after research is to verify, verify and verify. Since Nigeria is not particularly the first investment destination on the minds of millions of Americans, doesn't it make sense for you to verify all the information that your broker is providing you with? With the negative "419" reputation the country has, taking the time to investigate companies, auditors and other information available should not be considered an inconvenience but the responsibility of a smart investor. Contact regulatory agencies such as the SEC, NSE and the Corporate Affairs Commission (CAC) if you need more information on the status of a certain company or business venture. A good resource for all foreign investors is the Nigerian Investment Promotion Council (NIPC), a government agency that provides free information on various investment opportunities in the country; including the domestic stock market. As you invest in Nigeria, always be aware that it is your money at work and although there are great professionals that make the process easier for you, never take your eyes off the ball.

As you explore this emerging market, use the information provided in this book, develop the mind of a financial analyst and engage in a challenging cross-Atlantic investment program; I wish you success, few tears and a lot of money. Go get it!

APPENDIX A: GLOSSARY

African Banking Corporation (ABC): First bank to operate in Nigeria. Formed by a consortium of British banks in 1892, its headquarters was in London but all its branches were located abroad

Abuja: Nigerian capital city located in the middle of the country

Accountant: Qualified professional who after rigorous financial training practices accounting, which involves the maintenance and auditing of the financial books of an organization

American Depositary Receipt (ADR): Stock certificates issued by a US based depositary bank to shareholders, representing a certain amount of foreign shares held by the issuing bank

Advanced Fee Fraud: Also known as the 419 scam after the section of the Nigerian penal code that it violates, it is a criminal technique of obtaining money under false pretext from a victim by requesting them to pay an upfront fee to partake in a huge fortune. The scam artists are commonly called **Yahoo Boys** in Nigeria

Analyst Rating: The recommendation of a financial analyst to investors on whether to buy, sell or hold the stock of a specific company

Annual Report: The annual statements of a corporation's financial operations. The annual report includes vital information captured in the balance sheet, income statement, cash flow statement, auditor's report and management discussion

Appreciation: The increase in value of an asset

Arbitrage: The simultaneous buying and selling of an asset by experienced speculators in a bid to make a gain from the price differential of the asset in two different markets

Asian Tigers: Term economists coined that refers to the economies of Hong Kong, South Korea, Singapore and Taiwan for their rapid industrialization and high economic growth rates between the 1960s and 1990s

Asset: Any resource of economic value that a person, government or business has ownership rights over and expects to generate future benefit

Automated Trading System (ATS): An electronic stock transaction system that books the buy and sell orders of investors on the Nigerian Stock Exchange

Audit: An independent and unbiased review of the financial statements of an organization. Conducted by internal or external audit teams, its primary role is to determine the accuracy and financial responsibility of the specific organization

Balance Sheet: A financial statement that shows the assets, liabilities and net worth of a company at any given time

Bankruptcy: The inability of an individual or corporation to meet their or its financial obligations to creditors

Barclays Bank: One of the largest banks in the United Kingdom founded in 1690 that has an extensive network in developing countries

British Bank of West Africa (BBWA): Overseas British bank that took over the operations of the defunct African Banking Corporation and is credited with the introduction of modern banking in former British colonies in West Africa

Bear Market: A market characterized by a rapid fall in the prices of company stocks

Berlin Conference: Infamous meeting hosted by Germany between 1884 and 1885 where fourteen European nations gathered to divide the African continent into colonial territories for themselves. The final communiqué of the conference, the General Act of the Berlin Conference, is labeled by scholars as the official document of the *Scrabble for Africa*

Bloomberg: American Media Corporation that provides global financial news and data to financial corporations and other organizations around the world

Boiler Room: A location where stockbrokers use dishonest sales tactics to lure prospective investors into buying stocks in fraudulent, little known and often unsubstantiated companies. Brokerages that operate boiler rooms traditionally hold large stakes in the stock and intend selling the stock at a high price to brokerage clients, normally discouraging investors from researching the company because of time constraints

Bond: A financial debt instrument issued by corporations and governments to borrow funds from investors that pays a fixed sum annually as interest until maturity and then pays back the initial principal invested

Bureau of Public Enterprises (BPE): Nigerian government agency responsible for the privatization and commercialization of state-owned enterprises

Broad Street: street in downtown Lagos that hosts the largest financial district in Nigeria, the equivalent of New York City's Wall Street

Brokerage: A company involved in the purchase and sale of securities on behalf of its investor clients. Also referred to as the commission paid to a broker-dealer for executing a buy or sell transaction

Bull Market: A market characterized by rising stock prices

Business Fundamentals: Relevant financial information that focuses on the revenue, earnings, cash flow, assets, liabilities and general growth of a company; used to aid an investment decision

Business Model: The strategic plan formulated by the management of a company that shows it generates revenue, controls cost and makes a profit

Corporate Affairs Commission (CAC): Nigerian government agency that regulates the formation and management of companies

Capacity Utilization: Business and economic concept that measures the level to which a company maximizes the installed productive capacity available for its operations

Capital Market: Regulated market where corporations and governments source long-term financing by issuing stocks and bonds

Cash Account: An account held by an investor with a brokerage where transactions in stocks and bonds are settled on a cash basis

Cash Flow Statement: A vital part of a company's annual report that is submitted quarterly and annually to financial regulators detailing the inflow and outflow of cash from its financial, business and operating activities

Central Bank of Nigeria (CBN): Apex bank in Nigeria that is responsible for the issuance of the legal tender currency, maintenance of external reserves, implementation of the nation's monetary and fiscal policies, while serving as banker and financial adviser to the Federal Government

Chartered Financial Analyst (CFA): Globally reputed professional designation accorded individuals who pass rigorous financial analysis examinations conducted by the US based CFA Institute.

Chartered Institute of Stockbrokers (CIS): Professional body granted statutory powers that regulates the practice of stock broking in Nigeria. It offers a mandated examination program for any individual seeking to transact buy or sale orders on the Nigerian Stock Exchange.

CNBC: American media company covering business news and financial markets in major trading markets

Cold Calling: A sales tactic used by businesses to approach prospective clients, without solicitation from the target individual

Collateral: An asset, usually financial or tangible, used to secure a debt obligation

Commission: Fee charged by a stockbroker in exchange for services rendered

Conglomerate: A large corporation comprised of many companies operating in different businesses. The diverse business structure of conglomerates enables diversification which minimizes business risk

Corporate Raider: Businessperson who seeks controlling stake in a publicly traded company by purchasing or attempting to purchase a significant amount of stock in the company, usually in opposition to the wishes of the target company's management

Central Securities Clearing System (CSCS): Subsidiary of the Nigerian Stock Exchange that serves as the clearing house for all quoted share transactions in Nigeria, facilitating the transfer of and payment for shares amongst investors

Currency Risk: Risk that occurs due to the price changes between two currencies. Investors with investments in a foreign country face this risk, since changes in the value of the foreign currency relative to the currency of the investor's own country will determine if they gain or lose on the investment when the foreign investment is converted back to the investor's currency

Debt: A specific amount of money owed by an individual, corporation or government to another party

Depreciation: The decrease in value of an asset

Discount Broker: Stockbroker who trades stocks without providing investment advice to clients, charging lower commissions as compared to full service brokers

Discount House: Financial institution that trades in money market securities issued by the government such as treasury bills and certificates and commercial bills, issued by corporations

Diversification: A risk reduction technique that involves spreading investments in various assets; including real estate, mutual funds, stocks, cash and bonds

Dividend: A share of profits earned by a corporation distributed to investors

Economic and Financial Crimes Commission (EFCC): Independent law enforcement agency responsible for the investigation of economic and financial crimes in Nigeria. Designated a Financial Intelligence Unit (FIU), it coordinates the activities of joint task forces comprising of other law enforcement bodies in crippling money laundry crimes in the country

Emerging Market: Economic term used to describe countries in the transitional phase between developing and developed economy status. Most emerging markets are characterized by increasing low-to-middle income levels, the growth of industrial corporations, deregulated economic and financial policies, and increase in local and foreign investment

Enron: American energy trading and utilities company that crumbled as a result of the largest accounting fraud in history. Once ranked as the seventh largest corporation in the United States, senior executives of the company in collusion with its auditors applied fraudulent accounting practice to inflate company revenue figures. After regulatory investigation brought the fraud to light, Enron filed for Chapter 11 bankruptcy on December 2, 2001

Exchange-Traded Fund (ETF): Security instrument that tracks an index fund containing a number of listed stocks and trades like a stock on the stock exchange. Popular amongst investors in advanced economies, exchange-traded funds offer the benefits of diversification and lower transactions cost relative to mutual funds

Exotic Stock: Term referring to stocks of companies located in emerging markets

Financial Advisor: Finance professionals that help individuals develop short and long-term financial plans and recommend investments that enable their clients achieve their financial goals. Some financial advisors specialize in specific areas such as retirement planning, college funding, risk management, taxes and estate planning

Financial Analysis: The examination and review of the financial statements of a business so as to assess its true financial condition, economic prospects and determine its viability as a worthwhile investment

Federal Inland Revenue Service (FIRS): Federal agency responsible for tax collection and tax law enforcement in Nigeria

Generally Accepted Accounting Principles (GAAP): A set of accounting standards, principles and procedures that acts as guidelines for financial accounting amongst American companies, ensuring a minimum level of consistency in the preparation of financial statements

Globalization: Common term or phenomenon describing the interdependency of people and companies in different locations as a result of economic, social and technological change in the contemporary world. Effective globalization is achieved by the integration of marketing insight, technological innovation and languages in a business where those resources are no longer restricted to one specific location

House Stock: Stock of a company that stockbrokers in a brokerage are instructed to aggressively sell to investors, since the company management will receive an undisclosed profit from the company or have a significant stake in the company

Ibadan: Largest indigenous city in Sub-Saharan Africa, located 78 miles north of Lagos

Institute of Chartered Accountants of Nigeria (ICAN): Professional body granted statutory powers to regulate the practice of accounting in Nigeria

Income Statement: Important financial document that provides a summary of the revenue generated, expenses incurred and profit or loss of a company in a specified accounting period. Also known as a Profit and Loss statement, its primary aim is to indicate the financial performance of the company

Income Stock: Term referring to a stock that has had a consistent track record of paying out dividends, which constitute a significant component of the stock's total return on investment

Insider: General term for an individual who has access to valuable information on a company that is not public knowledge. In other instances, it refers to an investor that holds more than 10% of a company's total stock

Institutional Investor: A corporate entity that engages in securities transactions in large amounts that qualify them for lower commissions and preferential treatment. Most institutional investors are insurance companies, mutual and pension funds

Interest Rate Risk: The risk that the value of an investment will change in absolute terms due to a change in interest rates. Such changes affect stock prices, particularly in the event of rising interest rates

Investable Funds: Part of income set aside for investment purposes

Investment Bank: Financial institution that prepares securities for sale on behalf of governments and corporations, undertake mergers and acquisitions and underwrites the securities of issuing companies. The underwriting role of investment banks involves the investment bank working with the issuer of securities to determine the offering price, buys them from the issuer and sells them through an extensive distribution network

Investment Risk: Uncertainty of the future value of an investment made today

Issuing House: Financial institutions that advice corporations on how to source financing from the stock exchange and helps them meet statutory guidelines to be listed on the stock exchange

Joint Venture Agreement (JVA): A strategic alliance between two or more persons or corporations to undertake a particular business venture, each member of the venture agreeing to share profits, loss and control of the venture

Kano: Third largest city and economic center of the Northern part of Nigeria

Lagos: Largest city in Nigeria and commercial hub of the West African sub-region

Liabilities: The financial and legal obligations a corporation incurs during the normal course of business

Liquidation: A process that occurs when a corporation undergoes bankruptcy. Upon the termination of the business, company assets are sold and the proceeds paid to creditors. The remnants of the proceeds are distributed to shareholders

Liquidity: Ability of an asset to be converted into cash easily and quickly without a discount on the value of the asset. Assets with liquidity are characterized by their marketability and high level of trading activity in real and financial markets

Margin Account: A brokerage account in which an investor borrows cash from a broker-dealer to purchase securities. The loan is structured as a cash and securities-based collateral to safeguard the interests of the broker

Market Capitalization: Total size and value of a publicly traded company. It is calculated by multiplying the number of outstanding shares times the current market price of the company's stock

Market Maker: A broker-dealer that assumes the risk of holding a significant stake of stocks in a company so as to facilitate trading in that particular stock. Market makers quote both buy and sell orders for an asset

Maverick Investor: Individual investor who exhibits an aversion to conventional investment philosophy

Money Market Association of Nigeria (MMAN): Independent body that regulates the practice of money management in Nigeria and provides economic research and information to the investing public

Multinational Corporation (MNC): A corporation that has assets and business operations in a country other than its own. Sometimes called transnational corporations, multinationals usually have a head office in the originating country from where they coordinate their global operations

Money Market: Regulated securities market where dealing in short-term debt and monetary instruments is conducted. Instruments traded mature in less than one year and exhibit a high level of liquidity

Mutual Fund: An investment management company that collects money from a group of investors and reinvests those funds in stocks, bonds and other securities; as a means of achieving diversification. Each investor in the mutual fund owns shares in the company, representing a portion of the holdings of the fund

National Insurance Commission (NAICOM): Apex body that regulates and sets standards for the insurance industry in Nigeria

National Accounting Standards Board (NASB): Independent body in Nigeria responsible for the development and issuance of Statements of Accounting Standards for users and preparers of financial statements, investors, commercial enterprises and regulatory agencies of government

Niger Delta: Swampy region in southern Nigeria located at the delta of the River Niger, where 75% of Nigerian oil is produced

Nigerian Investment Promotion Council (NIPC): Government agency established to help local and foreign investors overcome bureaucratic hindrances to doing business in Nigeria and promote investment opportunities abroad

NSE All-Share Index: A capitalization-weighted index, started in 1984, that is comprised of all corporations traded on the Nigeria Stock Exchange

Onitsha: Largest city and commercial center in Southeastern Nigeria and host to the largest market in West Africa

Overseas Private Investment Corporation (OPIC): American agency established to assist American-owned businesses invest in foreign countries. OPIC carries out its mandate by providing political and financial risk coverage for foreign direct investments in emerging markets

Price Earnings Ratio (P/E ratio): A method of stock valuation that compares the price of a stock to its per-share earnings. Calculated by dividing the market value per share by the earnings per share (EPS), the P/E ratio measures how cheap or expensive a stock so as to help the investor determine if a target company is undervalued or overvalued

Passive Income: Income earned by an individual from a rental property, business or other enterprise in which the individual is not actively involved

Political Risk: The financial risk that impacts the value of an investment due to a sudden change in the policies of a particular government

Port Harcourt: Administrative centre and capital city of the oil-rich Rivers state in Southern Nigeria. The largest city in the Niger Delta region, it hosts international oil exploration, production and service corporations

Privatization: The transfer of ownership and management of a government enterprise to a private corporation. Privatization is often implemented to improve efficiency and eliminate the bureaucratic tendencies common in many government-managed enterprises

Prospectus: Legal document offering securities for sale and providing details of a company's operations, corporate objectives, historical financial data and other information that could be considered vital to prospective investors

Ratio Analysis: Analysis and interpretation of the relationship between two or more financial variables in a company that helps investors and lenders make general assumptions on the financial condition of the specified company

Reuters: Global news service that provides reports to newspapers and broadcasters, with its core business being the supply of information and trading products to financial markets around the world

Revenue: Total amount of money a company receives from its business activities during a specific period. Revenue is calculated by multiplying the price of the goods or (and) services sold by the company by the quantity sold. In Europe and other parts of the world, revenue is called turnover

Risk Management: A method of identifying and analyzing various forms of risk, so as to mitigate the level of uncertainty in the investment decision-making process

Return on Assets (ROA): A ratio that indicates the profitability of a company relative to its assets. It is calculated by dividing the company's net income for the past twelve months by its total assets and the result shown as a percentage. ROA is considered a fair measure of how efficiently the company's management uses its assets to generate earnings

Return on Equity (ROE): A ratio that indicates the profitability of a company relative to the amount of money shareholders invested in the company. It is calculated by dividing the company's net income for the past twelve months by common shareholder equity and the result is shown as a percentage. ROE is considered a fair measure of how a company uses shareholders' money and its financial performance in comparison to other firms in the same industry

Return on Investment (ROI): A ratio that indicates the efficiency of a specific investment and determines if the existing or proposed investment is viable. It is calculated by dividing the return of the investment (gain from investment minus cost of investment) by the cost of the investment and the result is shown as a percentage. It is a significant measure of evaluating if management can justify committing funds into specific investments

Securities and Exchange Commission (SEC): Federal agency responsible for the regulation of capital market operations in Nigeria; with the primary role of protecting investors and facilitating capital formation

Shareholder Fatigue: Dissatisfaction amongst shareholders with the financial performance of a company and activities of management

Shareholder Equity: The amount of assets owned by a company's stockholders. It is a combination of the funds that were originally invested in the company and retained earnings which the company has accumulated through its business operations overtime

Speculator: A person who trades in stocks, bonds, commodities, currencies, real estate, derivatives or other valuable asset with a higher level of risk, in exchange for a higher-than-average profit. Traditionally experienced and sophisticated investors, speculators have a low aversion to risk and prefer large sum profits to steady streams of income

Stockbroker: A licensed person or financial institution that acts on behalf of investors to execute buy and sell orders on a stock exchange, charging a fee or commission for its services

Sub-Saharan Africa: Geographical area comprised of countries on the African continent that excludes North Africa

Trade Alert System (TAS): Electronic notification system that alerts subscribing investors on their mobile phones, on transaction activity on their trading accounts to prevent unauthorized trading

Trading Volume: The number of shares, bonds or contracts transacted during a given period of time

Transaction Cost: The cost of buying and selling assets, such as commissions and slippage

Transparency International: Brussels-based non-profit organization that monitors the level of transparency and accountability in countries around the world, encouraging governments to implement effective anti-corruption laws and policies

Underwriting: See **Investment Bank**

Unit Trust: A registered investment management company that pools funds from individual investors; purchases various assets and distributes profits to investors, rather than reinvesting them back in the funds. Although unit trusts share similar characteristics with mutual funds, there is a main distinction in that a mutual fund is actively managed by professional fund managers while unit trusts are not managed at all

Value Investor: Individual investor who buys stocks in companies they consider undervalued by the general market. The investing style of a value investor centers on selecting stocks that trade for less than their intrinsic value

Value Stock: A stock that appears attractive to investors because it tends to trade at a price lower than what fundamental analysis indicates, making it a target for value investors. Value stocks are characterized by high dividend yields and a book valuation that is high in relation to its stock price

***ValueLine* Survey**: Publication providing investment research on companies based in the United States

Value Added Tax (VAT): A consumption tax imposed on a good or service whenever value is added at a stage of production or service delivery and at the final sale. Considered an indirect sales tax in many economies, VAT is assessed at a flat rate of 5% of the value of goods and services supplied in Nigeria. Non-profit organizations are not exempt from the payment of VAT in Nigeria

Volatility: A statistical indicator of the dispersion of returns of a particular stock or index, which could cause a stock or index to rise or fall sharply within a specific period of time. From another perspective, volatility refers to the level of risk in the size of changes in a stock's value

Wall Street: Historic Street in lower Manhattan in New York that hosts the original NYSE building and headquarters of the largest US brokerages and investment banks. In common parlance, it refers to the financial and investment community in the United States

Yahoo Boys: Informal term in Nigeria referring to individuals who send scam letters using electronic email to unsuspecting foreigners in the infamous '419' scheme. See **Advanced Fee Fraud**

APPENDIX B: BROKERAGE FIRMS IN NIGERIA

BGL Securities Limited
Plot 1061, Abagbon Close, Victoria Island, Lagos.
Postal: P.O. Box 74122, Victoria Island- Lagos, Nigeria.
Telephone Numbers: (234)-1-2623257, 2623141, 2672799, 2672820
Fax Number: (234)-1-2623258
Email: info@bglltd.com
Website: www.bglltd.com
CEO: Albert Okumagba
Authorized Brokers: Albert Okumagba, Chibundu Edozie, Henry Laraiyetan, Charles Allah, Cornelius Oboh, Joel Okafor, Tony Nwozor and Sunday Adebola

UBA Securities Limited
97/105, Broad Street, (3rd & 4th Floor), Marina- Lagos.
Postal: P. O. Box 6492, Marina- Lagos, Nigeria.
Telephone: (234)-01-2667415, 2660792, 4612373, 2663806
Fax Number: (234)-1-2661154, 2667412
E-mail: ubasec@ubagroup.com
Website: www.ubagroup.com
CEO: Ben Nwaroh
Authorized Brokers: Bode Adesegha, Bawo Oritsejafor and Remi Olatunbode.

A.R.M. Investment Managers
1 Mekunwen Road,
Off Oyinkan Abayomi Drive,
Postal: P.O. Box 55765, Ikoyi- Lagos, Nigeria
Telephone: (234)-1-2692976, 2692097
Fax Number: (234)-1-2692835
E-mail: info@arm.com.ng
Website: www.arm.com.ng
CEO: Deji Alli

Securities Transactions & Trust Co. Limited
12th Floor, Foreshore Towers,
2A Osborne Road, Ikoyi- Lagos.
Postal: P. O. Box 51045, Ikoyi- Lagos, Nigeria
Telephone: (234)-1-2695479-81, 2694005, 2690861
Fax Number: (234)-1-2694392
Email: enquiries@sectrust.com
Website: www.sectrust.com
CEO: Godwin N. Obaseki
Authorized Brokers: Godwin Obaseki, Jude Chiemeka, Victor Agbesoyin and Kenneth Nwafor.

IBTC Asset Management Limited
I.B.T.C. Place, Walter Carrington Crescent, Victoria Island, Lagos.
Postal: P. O. Box 71707, Victoria Island- Lagos, Nigeria.
Telephone: (234)-1-2626520-40
Fax Number: (234)-1-2626541/2
E-mail: assetmanagement@ibtclagos.com
Website: ibtc@ibtc.com
CEO: Yinka Sanni
Authorized Brokers: Yinka Sanni, Obinnia Abajue, Akeem Oyewale and Laolu Martins

Nigerian Stockbrokers Limited
NAL Towers, 13th Floor, 20 Marina Street,
Postal: P.M.B.12659, Lagos, Nigeria.
Telephone: (234)-1-2646837, 2635539, 4754007, 4755007, 2600420-9
Fax Number: (234)1-2645477.
E-mail: nsl@nalbank.com
Website: www.nigerianstockbrokerslimited.com
CEO: Bosun Adekoya
Authorized Brokers: Bosun Adekoya and Ayodeji Akinola

Zenith Securities Limited
84, Ajose Adeogun Street,
Victoria Island, Lagos.
Postal: P.O. Box 75315, Victoria Island- Lagos, Nigeria.
Telephone: (234)-1-2700436, 2700437
Fax Number: (234)-1-2703200
Email: enquiries@zenithsecuritiesng.com
Website: www.zenithsecuritiesng.com
CEO: Ben-Andrew Agbo
Authorized Brokers: Mohammed Garuba and Yomi Ogunfowora

Counter Trust Securities Limited
Niger House, 7th Floor,
1/5 Odunlami Street,
P. M. B. 12913, Lagos.
Telephone: (234)-1-2640160- 9, 2640181
Fax Number: (234)-1-2640171, 2640173-4
E-mail: info@counterstrust.com
Website: www.counterstrust.com
CEO: Aigboje Higo (Jnr.)
Authorized Brokers: Aigboje Higo (Jnr.), Samson Amedu, Chinenye Kene-Okafor and Amos Aledare.

Amyn Investments Limited
19th Floor, Stock Exchange House,
2/4 Customs Street, Lagos.
Postal: P. O. Box 2911, Marina, Lagos.
Telephone: (234)-1-2643973
Fax Number: (234)-1-2662043
E-mail: info@amyninvestments.com
Website: www.amyninvestments.com
CEO: Hauwa Macjad Audu
Authorized Brokers: Hauwa Audu, Monday Usiade and Patrick Eghiegbai Umoru.

Cashcraft Asset Management Limited
Foreshore Towers,
2A, Osborne Road, Ikoyi,
Postal: P. M. B. 80105, Victoria Island, Lagos.
Telephone/Fax: 234-01-2694287-9, 2701679, 4612207.
E-mail: lagos@cashcraft.com
Website: www.cashcraft.com
CEO: Adeolu Ireyomi

Authorized Brokers: Adeolu Ireyomi, Anthony Ikpea, Clement Ukogu, Agbola Abolade and Emmanuel Iseghohimen.

Centre-Point Investments & Securities Ltd
Nicon House, 4th Floor,
5, Customs Street, Lagos.
Postal: P. O. Box 1271, Lagos, Nigeria.
Telephone: (234)-1-2669913, 2643177
Fax Number: (234)-1-2643177.
CEO: Dr. J. O. Ologun.
Authorized Brokers: Dennis Odife, M. Muomah and J. O. Ologun.

Denham Management Limited
New Africa House,
31, Marina, Lagos.
Postal: P.O. Box 4454, Lagos- Nigeria.
Telephone: (234)-1-2644641, 2664445, 4731800
Fax Number: (234)-1-2661763
E-mail: info@denham-management.com
Website: www.denham-management.com
CEO: Gamaliel Onosode, Jnr.
Authorized Brokers: Gamaliel Onosode, Jnr. and Joel Okoedion

CSL Stockbrokers Limited
Primrose Tower, 4th Floor,
17A Tinubu Street, Lagos.
Postal: P. O. Box 9117, Lagos, Nigeria.
Telephone: (234)-1-2665944-53, 2641293, 2641297
Fax Number: (234)-1-2662033;
E-mail: research@firstcitygroup.com
Website: www.csl-group.com
Authorized Brokers: Sunny Anene, Tom La'ah, Idika Kalu Uma and Confidence Onwuka

Lead Securities and Investment Limited
Plot 281 Ajose Adeogun Street,
Victoria Island, Lagos.
Telephone: (234)-1-2629732, 2615186, 2922907
Fax Number: (234)-1-2618428.
E-mail: info@leadcapitalng.com
Website: www.leadcapitalng.com
CEO: Yemisi Tayo-Aboaba
Authorized Brokers: Oluwaseyin Abe, Oluwasegun Oye, Olaolu Dada and Busola Awosanya.

Intercontinental Securities Limited
Bull Plaza, 16th Floor,
38/39 Marina, Lagos.
Telephone: (234)-1-2665592, 2669489, 2702282
Fax Number: (234) 1 2667165.
E-mail: isl@intersecltd.com
Website: www.intersecltd.com
CEO: Oluwole O. Adeosun

Authorized Brokers: Oluwole O. Adeosun and Bamidele A. Abdul.

Strategy and Arbitrage Limited
Bull Plaza, 18th Floor,
38/39 Marina, Lagos.
Telephone: (234)-1-2660233, 2668702, 4719043, 08023030499
Fax: (234)-1-2702296.
E-mail: info@strategy-arbitrage.com
Website: www.strategy-arbitrage.com
CEO: Tony Anonyai.
Authorized Brokers: James B. Akpan

Stanbic Equities Nigeria Limited
Stanbic House,
Plot 688, Amodu Tijani Close,
Victoria Island, Lagos.
Postal: P. O. Box 54746, Falomo- Lagos, Nigeria.
Telephone: (234)-1-2709660-99, 08033085461
Fax Number: (234)-1-2709667
Email: enquiries@stanbic.com
Website: www.stanbic.com
CEO: Folajimi Kuti
Authorized Brokers: Folajimi Kuti, Sotubo O. George and Prince Adegbite.

TRW Stockbrokers Limited
62/64, 5th Floor,
Campbell Street, Lagos.
Postal: G. P. O. Box 3233, Marina- Lagos, Nigeria.
Telephone: (234)-1-2646976, 2646999, 2600786
Fax Number: (234)-1-2637743
Website: www.trw-stockbrokers.com
CEO: Azubuike Okpalaoka
Authorized Brokers: Azubuike Okpalaoka and Abdul-Rasheed Momoh.

Union Stockbrokers Limited
4, Davies Street, Off Marina, Lagos.
Telephone: (234)-1-2667541, 2668484, 2667313
Fax Number: (234)-1-2660874, 2662803
E-mail: unionmbl@micro.com.ng
CEO: Niyi Opeodu
Authorized Brokers: Niyi Opeodu, Segun Bamigboye and Shehu Elakama.

Vetiva Capital Management
Plot 266B, Kofo Abayomi Street,
Victoria Island, Lagos.
Telephone: (234)-1-4617521-3
Fax Number: (234)-1-4617524
Email: info@vetiva.com
Website: www.vetiva.com
CEO: Chuka Eseka

APPENDIX C: REGULATORY BODIES IN NIGERIA

Securities and Exchange Commission
Labour House Building (5th -9th Floor)
Central Business District,
P.M.B. 315, Garki – Abuja,
Federal Capital Territory.
Telephone: (234)-9-2346272-3
Fax: (234)-9-2346276
E-Mail: sechq@secngr.org
Website: www.secngr.org

Nigerian Stock Exchange
(8th, 9th, & 11th Floors)
2/4 Customs Street,
P.O. Box 2457, Lagos,
Telephone: (234)-1-2660287, 2660305, 2660335
Telex: 23567 STEX NIG.
Fax: (234)-1-2668724, 2668281
Email: info@nigerianstockexchange.com
Website: www.nigerianstockexchange.com

Central Bank of Nigeria
Zaria Street, Cadastral Zone
Central Business District
P.M.B. 0187, Garki- Abuja, Federal Capital Territory.
Telephone: (234)-9-961639701-2
Fax: (234)-9-61636012
Email: info@cenbank.org
Website: www.cenbank.org

Central Securities Clearing System Limited
2/4 Customs Street, Stock Exchange House
P O Box 2457, Marina, Lagos
Telephone: (234)-1-2664075, 2643007, 2643139
Fax: (234)-1-2664058
Website: www.cscsdepository.com

The Institute of Chartered Accountants of Nigeria
Plot 16, Idowu Taylor Street,
Victoria Island, P.O. Box 1580,Lagos.
Telephone: (234)-1-2617638, 2614235, 2622393
Fax: (234)-1-2610304
E-mail: info.ican@ican.org.ng
Website: www.ican.org.ng

The Chartered Institute of Taxation in Nigeria
(3rd & 4th Floors) Don De Dieu Plaza,
11, Ikorodu Road (Opposite CPI-Moore),
Maryland, Lagos.
Telephone: (234)-1-774-1273, 493-5054
Fax: (234)-1-4935059
Email: citn@citn.org
Website: www.citn.org

The Chartered Institute of Stockbrokers
Stock Exchange House,
Level 15, 2/4 Customs Street, Lagos
Telephone: (234)-1-2663146, 2663921, 2661049
Fax: (234)-1-2660986
Email: cis@nova.net.ng
Website: www.cisnigeria.com

The Chartered Institute of Bankers in Nigeria
Bankers House Building
PC 19, Adeola Hopewell Street,
P. O. Box 72273
Victoria Island, Lagos.
Telephone: (234)-1-2617674, 611306, 7749364, 4617924, 8128696, 615642, 615792
Fax: (234)-1-4618930
Email: cibn@cibnnigeria.org
Website: www.cibnnigeria.org

Nigerian Accounting Standard Boards
Elephant Cement House (3rd Floor)
ASSBIFI Road, Alausa,
P.O.Box 10968
Ikeja, Lagos Nigeria.
Telephone: (234)-1-791779, 4812099
Fax: (234)-1-3451150, 5546296
Website: www.nig-asb.com

APPENDIX D: IMPORTANT GOVERNMENT AGENCIES

Nigerian Investment Promotion Commission
Plot 1181 Aguiyi Ironsi Street
Maitama District
P.M.B. 381 Garki Abuja,
Federal Capital Territory.
Telephone: (234)-9-4134380, 4131403, 4134112, 4130582
Fax: (234)-9-4134112
Email: nipc@nipc-nigeria.org
Website: www.nipc-nigeria.org

Federal Ministry of Finance
Ahmadu Bello Way, Central Area,
P.M.B. 14, Garki, Abuja
Federal Capital Territory.
Telephone: (234)-9-2346290-5
Website: www.fmf.gov.ng

Bureau of Public Enterprises
The Presidency
1 Osun Crescent, Maitama,
Abuja, Federal Capital Territory.
Telephone: (234)-9-4134636 - 46
Fax: (234)-9-4134657, 4134671 - 2
Email: askbpe@bpeng.org
Website: www.bpeng.org

National Deposit Insurance Commission
Plot 447/448 Constitution Avenue
P.M.B. 284, Garki- Abuja,
Federal Capital Territory.
Telephone: (234)-9-5237710-21
Fax: (234)-9-5237718
E-mail: info@ndic-ng.com
Website: www.ndic-ng.com

National Pension Commission
Plot 2774, Shehu Shagari Way,
Maitama District, P.M.B. 5170,
Wuse, Federal Capital Territory.
Telephone: (234)-9-4138736-40
Fax: (234)-9-413363
E-mail: info@pencom.gov.ng
Website: www.pencom.gov.ng

Nigerian Communications Commission
Plot 72, Ahmadu Bello Way, Central Business District,
Benue Plaza, Abuja, Federal Capital Territory.
Telephone: (234)-9-2340330, 2344589
Email: ncc@ncc.gov.ng
Website: www.ncc.gov.ng

Nigerian National Petroleum Corporation
NNPC Towers, Central Business District,
Herbert Macaulay Way, P.M.B. 190,
Garki- Abuja,
Federal Capital Territory.
Telephone: (234)-9-2348200-17, 20081000-6
Fax: (234)-9-2340029
Cablegram: Napetcor
Website: www.nnpcgroup.com

Corporate Affairs Commission
Plot 565, Ndola Square,
P.M.P 198, Garki- Abuja,
Federal Capital Territory.
Telephone: (234)-9-5241046-50
Fax: (234)-9-5241015
Email: cservice@cac.gov.ng
Website: www.cac.gov.ng

Federal Inland Revenue Service
Plot 522, Sokode Crescent,
Off Dalaba Street, Wuse Zone 5,
P.M.B. 33, Garki- Abuja,
Federal Capital Territory
Telephone: (234)-9-5236611
Fax: (234)-9-5239912
Email: enquiry@firs-nigeria.org
Website: www.firs-nigeria.org

APPENDIX E: LAW ENFORCEMENT CONTACTS

Economic and Financial Crimes Commission
Plot 1017-1018 Coree Bay Crescent,
Wuse II, Abuja,
Federal Capital Territory.
Telephone: (234)-9-6441000
Fax: (234)-9-3148074
Email: info@efccnigeria.com
Scam Mail Box: scam@efccnigeria.org
Website: www.efccnigeria.com

Nigerian Police Force
Force Headquarters
Louis Edet House
Shehu Shagari Way
Area 11 Garki, Abuja,
Federal Capital Territory.
Telephone: (234)-9-234 0633, 234 0422
Fax: (234)-9-2340422
Website: www.nigerianpolice.org

Federal Investigation & Intelligence Bureau
Special Fraud Unit
Alagbon Close, Ikoyi, Lagos.
Telephone: (234)-1-680067, 686292

United States Secret Service
Financial Crimes Division
245 Murray Drive,
Building 410,
Washington, DC 20223
Telephone: (1)-202-406-5708
Website: www.secretservice.gov

Embassy of the Federal Republic of Nigeria
Security and Defence Attaches
3519 International Court, NW
Washington, DC 20008
Telephone: (1)-202-986-8400
Fax: (1)-202-775-1385
Website: www.nigeriaembassyusa.org

APPENDIX F: ECONOMIC & FINANCIAL RESEARCH FIRMS

SBA Research Group
Suite 25408
72 New Bond street
London, United Kingdom
W1S 1RR
Telephone: +44 (0) 208 557 1350
Fax: +44 (0) 208 557 1350
Email: customerservices@sbaresearch.com
Website: www.sbaresearch.com

Agusto and Company Limited
UBA House (5th Floor),
57 Marina, P.O .Box 56136,
Falomo, Ikoyi- Lagos, Nigeria.
Telephone: (234)-1-2643571-5
Email: info@agusto.com
Website: www.agusto.com

Economic Associates
31, Akin Adesola Street,
Victoria Island, Lagos, Nigeria.
Telephone: (234)-1-4610800-4
Fax: (234)-1-4610805
Email: info@econassociates.com
Website: www.econassociates.com

African Business Research Limited
Unit 1-2, Universal House,
88-94, Wentworth Street,
London, United Kingdom
E1 7SA
Telephone: +44 (0)20 7392 4058
Fax: +44 (0)20 7392 4059
Email: info@africanbusinessresearch.com
Website: www.africanbusinessresearch.com

CMC International Limited
6, Ajele Street, Off Campbell Street, Lagos Island,
P.O.Box 2708, Apapa, Lagos, Nigeria.
Telephone: (234)-1-2645846, 2645847, 2645845
Fax: (234)-1-2645844
Email: cmc@cmcint.com
Website: www.cmcint.com

APPENDIX G: ONLINE RESOURCES

The Guardian
www.ngrguardiannews.com

This Day
www.thisdayonline.com

Financial Standard Magazine
www.financialstandardnews.com

Business Day
www.businessdayonline.com

Nigeria World
www.nigeriaworld.com

African Capital Markets Watch
www.africancapitalmarkets.com

All Africa Magazines
www.allafrica.com

APPENDIX H: LIST OF PUBLICLY TRADED COMPANIES
All Values in Naira as at 08-18-2006 ($1=N131.55)

	SHARE PRICE	MARKET CAPITALIZATION
AGRICULTURE		
ELLAH LAKES PLC	0.50	30,000,000.00
GROMMAC INDS. PLC	0.38	15,200,000.00
LIVESTOCK FEEDS PLC	0.95	23,522,699.20
OKITIPUPA OIL PALM PLC	0.95	68,400,000.00
OKOMU OIL PALM PLC	38.82	12,343,595,400.00
PRESCO PLC	15.33	7,665,000,000.00
AIRLINE		
ALBARKAIR	0.61	1,830,000,000.00
ADC	1.02	04,000,000.00
AUTOMOBILE & TYRE		
DUNLOP NIGERIA PLC	2.52	1,905,120,000.00
INCAR NIGERIA PLC	3.40	1,139,000,000.00
INTRA MOTORS PLC	0.57	17,100,000.00
R T BRISCOE PLC	8.94	3,245,863,680.00
RIETZCOT NIGERIA CO. PLC	0.65	83,200,000.00
BANKING		
ACB INTERNATIONAL BANK	0.94	4,700,000,000.00
ACCESS BANK NIGERIA PLC	2.94	42,689,781,489.60
AFRIBANK NIGERIA PLC	9.00	45,975,899,988.00
COOPERATIVE BANK PLC	1.92	5,760,000,000.00
DIAMOND BANK NIGERIA PLC	6.61	50,259,813,946.15
ECOBANK PLC	8.74	189,257,943,333.24
EKO INTERNATIONAL BANK PLC	2.26	18,646,043,670.26
FIDELITY BANK PLC	2.54	41,478,609,064.46
FIRST BANK OF NIGERIA. PLC	43.59	228,413,186,489.38
FIRST CITY MONUMENT BANK	4.99	47,653,319,740.25

FIRST INLAND	3.62	35,072,839,094.08
GUARANTY TRUST BANK PLC	17.99	143,920,000,000.00
GUARDIAN EXPRESS BANK PLC	1.51	14,803,205,919.79
INTERCONTINENTAL BANK PLC	16.13	172,973,396,281.11
IBTC CHARTERED BANK PLC	6.40	77,166,130,899.20
NAL MERCHANT BANK PLC	2.80	11,173,470,777.00
OCEANIC	14.24	132,625,739,472.00
OMEGA BANK (NIGERIA) PLC	1.91	5,921,653,097.76
PLATINUMHABIB BANK PLC	2.40	46,332,179,520.00
SKYE BANK PLC	3.06	33,890,641,462.62
TRANS INTERNATIONAL BANK PLC	0.36	1,440,000,000.00
U.B.A PLC.	22.50	158,850,000,000.00
UNION BANK NIG. PLC	29.50	175,993,066,647.00
UNITY BANK PLC	2.50	17,420,086,040.00
UNIVERSAL TRUST BANK	0.48	1,122,777,596.16
WEMA BANK PLC	3.33	32,001,463,689.48
ZENITH BANK PLC	25.60	153,600,000,000.00

BREWERIES

CHAMPION BREWERIES. PLC	2.38	2,142,000,000.00
GOLDEN GUINEA BREW.PLC	0.68	92,534,400.00
GUINNESS NIG PLC	157.00	185,250,645,155.00
INTERNATIONAL BREWERIES PLC	0.87	359,235,772.47
JOS INT. BREWERIES PLC.	3.43	577,955,000.00
NIGERIAN BREW PLC.	49.30	372,834,323,362.00
PREMIER BREWERIES PLC.	0.93	117,180,000.00

BUILDING MATERIALS

ASHAKA CEM. PLC	51.49	75,304,125,000.00
BENUE CEMENT COMPANY PLC	12.18	6,029,100,000.00
CEMENT CO. OF NORTH NIG. PLC	10.74	11,472,612,141.54
CERAMIC MANUFACTURER NIG. PLC	0.25	30,851,000.00
NIGER CEM. PLC	5.00	556,747,890.00
NIGERIAN ROPES PLC.	2.81	745,800,076.80

NIGERIAN WIRE INDUSTRIES	2.24	33,600,000.00
W.A. PORTLAND COMP. PLC.	56.00	168,089,600,224.00

CHEMICAL & PAINTS

AFRICAN PAINTS (NIGERIA) PLC	0.38	49,400,000.00
BERGER PAINTS PLC	3.00	652,102,755.00
CAP PLC	18.52	3,889,200,000.00
DN MEYER PLC	3.41	828,316,962.00
IPWA PLC	0.32	164,382,720.00
NIGERIA-GERMAN CHEMICALS PLC	5.30	815,065,863.60
PREMIER PAINTS PLC	0.67	41,875,000.00

COMMERCIAL/SERVICES

TRANS-NATIONWIDE EXPRESS PLC	0.57	57,000,000.00

COMPUTER & OFFICE EQUIPMENT

ATLAS NIGERIA PLC	0.13	2,263,978.08
HALLMARK PAPER PRODUCTS PLC	0.91	45,500,000.00
NCR (NIGERIA) PLC	3.00	324,000,000.00
THOMAS WYATT NIG. PLC	0.44	31,185,000.00
TRIPLE GEE AND COMPANY PLC	0.55	187,198,880.00
WIGGINS TEAPE NIGERIA PLC	0.95	76,950,000.00

CONGLOMERATES

A.G. LEVENTIS NIGERIA PLC	1.29	2,356,288,181.94
C.F.A.O. NIG. PLC	2.79	1,160,640,000.00
CHELLARAMS PLC	1.13	272,302,089.00
JOHN HOLT PLC	0.82	319,104,154.56
P.Z. INDUSTRIES PLC	28.06	71,303,414,970.54
S C O A NIG. PLC	0.38	276,285,333.08
U A C N PLC	31.70	40,594,110,210.00
U T C NIG. PLC	0.62	695,174,691.86
UNILEVER NIG. PLC	17.80	67,342,673,227.75

CONSTRUCTION

ARBICO PLC	1.31	194,535,000.00
CAPPA & D`ALBERTO PLC	10.45	2,057,354,200.00
COSTAIN (WA) PLC	1.31	183,933,825.00
G CAPPA PLC	2.00	250,000,000.00
JULIUS BERGER NIG PLC	32.73	9,819,000,000.00
ROADS NIG. PLC	1.03	20,600,000.00

ENGINEERING TECHNOLOGY

INTERLINKED TECHNOLOGIES PLC	1.21	45,831,416.84
NIGERIAN WIRE AND CABLE PLC.	0.46	193,200,000.00
ONWUKA HI-TEK INDUSTRIES PLC	0.10	6,817,239.80

FOOD/BEVERAGES & TOBACCO

7 UP BOTTLING COMP. PLC	52.30	21,441,823,250.00
BEVERAGES (WEST AFRICA) PLC	0.82	4,920,000.00
CADBURY NIGERIA PLC	70.00	77,058,986,620.00
FERDINAND OIL MILLS PLC	0.49	49,000,000.00
FLOUR MILLS NIG. PLC	63.49	73,953,152,000.00
FOREMOST DAIRIES PLC	0.51	2,263,762.50
NORTHERN NIGERIA FLOUR MILLS PLC	33.26	4,939,110,000.00
NATIONAL SALT CO. NIG. PLC	0.69	55,170,100.23
NESTLE FOODS NIGERIA PLC	254.10	134,275,968,750.00
NIG. BOTTLING CO. PLC	55.00	71,460,261,290.00
P S MANDRIDES & CO PLC	7.60	304,000,000.00
TATE INDUSTRIES PLC	0.21	13,977,824.91
UNION DICON SALT PLC	3.63	1,306,800,000.00

FOOTWEAR

FOOTWEAR AND ACCESSORIES MAN.	0.30	55,920,000.00
LENNARDS (NIG) PLC	0.59	41,396,796.58

HEALTHCARE

ABOSELDEHYDE LABS. PLC	0.59	30,503,000.00

BCN PLC	0.61	12,810,000.00
CHRIESTLIEB PLC	0.56	13,440,000.00
EKOCORP PLC	0.75	116,015,625.00
EVANS MEDICAL PLC	5.10	2,255,469,696.00
GLAXO SMITHKLINE	16.86	16,129,982,097.12
MAUREEN LABORATORIES PLC	0.27	18,360,000.00
MAY & BAKER NIGERIA PLC	5.20	1,242,274,594.70
MORISON INDUSTIES PLC	1.02	93,133,395.00
NEIMETH INTERNATIONAL PHARM	3.67	3,451,905,903.25
PHARMA - DEKO PLC	3.33	333,000,000.00

HOTEL & TOURISM

TOURIST COMPANY OF NIGERIA PLC	3.61	5,818,785,720.00

INDUSTRIAL/DOMESTIC PRODUCTS

ALUMINIUM EXTRUSION IND.PLC	2.08	208,000,000.00
ALUMINIUM MAN. OF NIG PLC	0.94	59,220,000.00
B.O.C. GASES PLC (IGL)	2.65	1,041,768,000.00
EPIC DYNAMICS PLC	0.40	48,000,000.00
FIRST ALUMINIUM NIGERIA PLC	0.65	807,163,600.75
LIZ-OLOFIN AND COMPANY PLC	0.64	32,000,000.00
NIG ENAMELWARE COMP. PLC	3.52	67,584,000.00
NIGERIAN LAMPS INDUST. PLC	0.28	28,000,000.00
NIYAMCO PLC	2.18	66,217,500.00
OLUWA GLASS COMPANY PLC	1.31	99,198,230.40
VITAFOAM NIG PLC	4.71	4,114,656,000.00
VONO PRODUCTS PLC	0.99	297,000,000.99

INSURANCE

ACEN INSURANCE PLC	1.00	600,000,000.00
AIICO INSURANCE PLC	1.91	2,674,000,000.00
AMICABLE ASSURANCE PLC	0.73	226,672,680.33
BAICO INSURANCE PLC	1.60	388,000,000.00
CONFIDENCE INSURANCE PLC	0.61	129,091,860.00

CORNERSTONE INSURANCE COMPANY	1.03	2,076,480,000.00
CRUSADER INSURANCE PLC	2.05	1,877,899,400.40
FIRST ASSURANCE PLC (TOWERGATE)	0.90	433,928,571.43
GREAT NIGERIAN INSURANCE PLC	1.72	2,580,000,000.00
GUINEA INSURANCE PLC	0.66	475,200,000.00
LASACO ASSURANCE PLC	0.90	1,270,080,000.00
LAW UNION AND ROCK INSURANCE PLC	1.58	1,580,000,000.00
LINKAGE ASSSURANCE PLC	1.45	3,827,986,470.05
MUTUAL BENEFITS ASSURANCE PLC	0.72	1,528,512,000.91
N.E.M INSURANCE CO (NIG) PLC	1.02	688,500,000.00
NFI ISURANCE	1.26	1,412,208,000.00
NIGER INSURANCE CO. PLC	3.10	6,200,000,000.00
PRESTIGE ASSURANCE CO. PLC	2.80	2,562,851,833.50
ROYAL EXCHANGE ASSURANCE PLC	2.85	4,565,157,471.15
SECURITY ASSURANCE PLC	0.81	145,800,000.00
STANDARD ALLIANCE INSURANCE PLC	1.30	1,911,000,000.00
SUN INSURANCE NIGERIA PLC	0.59	132,750,000.00
UNIC INSURANCE PLC	1.31	1,041,712,000.00
WEST AFRICAN PROV.INS.COY.PLC	3.09	3,089,999,998.76

MACHINERY (MARKETING)

BLACKWOOD HODGE (NIG) PLC	0.63	44,226,000.00
NIG. SEW. MACH. MAN. CO. PLC	0.15	882,000.00
STOKVIS NIG PLC	0.14	408,520.00

MANAGED FUNDS

C & I LEASING PLC	1.32	792,000,000.00
FIRST CAPITAL INV. TRUST PLC	0.45	27,000,000.00
NIGERIA ENERGY SECTOR FUND	761.00	1,902,500,000.00
NIGERIA INT. FUND PLC	6,897.51	1,103,601,600.00

MARITIME

JAPAUL OIL AND MARITIME SERVICES PLC	1.17	1,364,449,530.60

MORTGAGE COMPANIES

UNION HOMES SAVINGS AND LOANS PLC.	3.35	6,700,000,000.00

PACKAGING

ABPLAST PRODUCTS PLC	1.01	25,250,000.00
AVON CROWNCAPS & CONTAINER	0.98	558,579,198.52
BETA GLASS CO PLC	5.13	2,331,687,600.00
GREIF NIGERIA PLC	1.63	69,503,200.00
NAMPAK PLC	2.89	618,701,656.02
POLY PRODUCTS (NIG) PLC	0.48	115,200,000.00
STUDIO PRESS (NIG) PLC	1.54	86,240,000.00
W. A. GLASS IND. PLC	0.50	99,533,275.00

PETROLEUM(MARKETING)

AFRICAN PETROLEUM PLC	51.17	38,119,375,800.52
AFROIL PLC	0.43	46,127,464.82
CONOIL	85.74	35,290,584,000.00
ETERNA OIL & GAS PLC	2.20	999,199,999.60
MOBIL OIL NIG PLC	194.26	46,699,490,526.92
OANDO PLC	94.22	53,922,192,305.52
TEXACO (NIG) PLC	111.00	28,192,742,592.00
TOTAL NIGERIA PLC	205.00	69,601,976,585.00

PRINTING & PUBLISHING

ACADEMY PRESS PLC	1.23	247,968,000.00
DAILY TIMES PLC	0.69	16,560,000.00
LONGMAN NIGERIA PLC	5.93	1,046,052,000.00
UNIVERSITY PRESS PLC	3.00	437,367,417.00

REAL ESTATE

UACN PROPERTY DEVELOPMENT	12.40	13,640,000,000.00

TEXTILES

ABA TEXTILE MILLS PLC	0.91	144,274,657.80

AFPRINT NIGERIA PLC	0.55	283,623,283.35
ENPEE INDUSTRIES PLC	1.56	579,150,000.00
NIG. TEXTILE MILLS PLC	1.66	76,936,403.46
UNITED NIGERIA TEXTILES PLC	1.00	843,284,027.00
ASABA TEXTILE MILLS PLC	3.63	

SECOND-TIER SECURITIES

ADSWITCH PLC	1.55	193,758,137.50
AFRIK PHARMACEUTICALS PLC	0.45	11,204,482.50
ANINO INTERNATIONAL PLC	0.22	5,324,000.00
CAPITAL OIL PLC	0.34	31,386,876.96
CUTIX PLC	3.15	832,224,657.60
FLEXIBLE PACKAGING PLC	0.50	8,500,000.00
JULI PLC	0.52	101,244,000.00
KRABO NIGERIA PLC	0.13	5,094,375.00
NEWPAK PLC	1.05	44,375,992.50
RAK UNITY PET. COM. PLC	0.30	4,500,000.00
ROKANA INDUSTRIES PLC	0.48	14,400,000.00
SMART PRODUCTS NIGERIA PLC	1.45	26,100,000.00
TROPICAL PET. PRODUCTS PLC	0.29	4,234,000.00
UDEOFSON GARMENT FCT. NIG PLC	0.50	10,000,000.00
UNION VENTURES & PET. PLC	0.56	16,016,000.00
W.A. ALUMINIUM PRODUCTS PLC	0.50	3,325,000.00